for Matthew
hello –
?

Embarrassment of Survival

Paul Vangelisti

Edited by Standard Schaefer

Marsilio / Agincourt
New York . 2001

The author would like to thank the publishers of the books and periodicals in which some of these poems, written between 1970 and 2000, first appeared. Special thanks to John McBride for his invaluable help in first walking the invisible city, and to Luigi Ballerini for his belief in this and other projects.

This volume is dedicated to the memory of Adriano Spatola, Robert Zachary and Carolina Zangani who visit outrageously and often.

Copyright © Paul Vangelisti 2001
Introduction copyright © Standard Schaefer 2001
ISBN 1-56886-101-X

Book & Cover Design: Barbara Maloutas

Marsilio / Agincourt
PO Box 1039, Cooper Station
New York, NY 10003
marsiliopublishers.com

Contents

Introduction	by Standard Schaefer		7
Selected Poems	Written	Published	
Air	[1970-1973]	1973	17
The Extravagant Room	[1975]	1976	33
Portfolio	[1975-1976]	1978	43
Another You	[1978-1979]	1981	71
Gof in Singapore	[1982]	1983	89
Rime	[1983]	1984	99
Villa	[1983-1986]	1991	117
Alephs Again	[1988-1989]	1999	181
The Book of Life	[1989-1991]		187
Gold Mountain	[1996-1997]		265
Recent Poems	[1997-2000]		301
Notes			308
Bibliography			310

The product of Italian working class immigrants who received his education in the North Beach of San Francisco, Paul Vangelisti attended a French speaking grammar school. English was his second language. It is not surprising that a question of identity marks his work, but it is surprising that such concerns are relatively minimal. One is tempted to ask, "What is the opposite of identity?" His first book *Communion* (1970) suggested an answer, though the preoccupation with forms of communion gradually dissipated over the years into the more seemingly melancholy theme of exile. The tinge of estrangement present confounds the author's efforts to distinguish signs of individuality from the collage material, quotes and ordinary objects. The question becomes, "Is identity ever not a question of context?"

Neither a late beat nor an American surrealist of the sort common at the time in the academic presses, and certainly not a poet prone to expounding on poetic process, even in his early work Vangelisti asked if the focus on a decidedly personal poetry is not simply a revision of the expansionist, messianic strand of American pragmatism that allows Puritanism to live again as confessionalism. Personal psychology, the mind and consciousness struck him as pernicious abstractions that could only lead to a naive celebration of alienation, whether avowed or not. The second book, *Air*, also addressed the dangers of abstraction, particularly freedom, community and progress, terms that the title poem calls "words that no one can understand." The only possibility for subject matter remains the writer's daily, material existence, meaning that content is first and foremost the presentation of the context about which the poet can speak with some authority. Understandably, the first books of poetry were ideological, overtly political in their rhetoric and slightly vague in their own way. The realistic imagery, influenced in part by George Oppen, was offset by the occasional surrealistic flurry. Nevertheless, emphasis was on the physicality of the poem, its sense of place and concrete situations— all an attempt to overcome the abstractions so prevalent in the previous generation's political poems.

The realistic, fragmentary approach of this early period was no doubt partly the result of a young man imitating the style of his literary heroes like Jack Spicer, George Oppen, Ezra Pound and T.S. Eliot, but these exercises produced another unforeseen similarity: the book-length poem. For the most part, Vangelisti's individual pieces were unsatisfactory and not very promising as extensions of realism, especially if seen as independent and detached from the poems on the surrounding pages. Aesthetically, the first context one should note in Vangelisti's work is the specific book itself, even if the book is one of fragments. They are fragments "without anything lacking," as Marcel Proust might have said about such work as "Scapes," from *Another You*, or the title piece from *The Extravagant Room*. In such work, one is wisest not to look for what is missing, forgotten, repressed, but rather how each piece there deranges all the others. In this way, Vangelisti borrows techniques and forms from various traditions and yet completely alters the ideology behind those traditions. Seen in this manner, Vangelisti's surrealistic moments are actually a tacit resistance to the conviction that dreams, consciousness and existence were essentially synonyms. This is why his syntax seems to stutter at the precise moment when he is writing in a most overtly "poetic" manner.

By the mid-1970's, realism is more apparent, though it is a smooth, ethereal realism lacing together high and low source material, while not appearing resolutely incomplete. There was a musical quality emerging more clearly in this period, allowing the irrational aspects of reality to appear as if moving towards order, even if this order was only the music itself. Vangelisti became increasingly willing to change diction and syntax from the original sources in order to explore California's tenuous relationship to avant-gardism, and particularly West Coast jazz. The perception of the West as less sophisticated and less intellectual than the East may have contributed to his attempt to make the collage appear coherent, at least on the level of syntax. Like jazz, the next note surprises even as it affirms and confirms the earlier elements. Similarly, the disenfranchisement that Vangelisti shared with other Los Angeles poets like Stuart Z. Perkoff, John Thomas, Jack Hirschman or Charles Bukowski is always present, although it becomes a form of exile, one that allowed him to address the new, compound forms of immigrant experience, the ubiquitous lack of culture that repels and attracts people to Southern California. Perhaps here too is a clue to Vangelisti's being shunned by other American "experimentalists": if one does not have a monument, one need not deconstruct it.

This is not to say that his writing was not critical. It was, but it was also clinical in the sense linked to experiment. He was building from particular locales a notion of exile as an affect, mental but always inseparable from the physical. *Air*, for instance, the very title of which plays on the sense of the L.A. skyline as well as "heir", confronted the myth of possibility offered by California, its reputation as fertile and untenable. California as the embodiment of such clichés as the blank slate, the melting pot, the barren desert, and everything rootless comes ready-made with its own aesthetic. Forgetting is not simply a matter of losing history, but also avoiding geography. The brute force of physical obstacles, the physicality of the brutes living in the region allowed Vangelisti's West to be dialectically opposed to East Coast dandyism. Vangelisti's West is neither a source of intellectual pragmatism, nor a place where truth is revealed to the mind that contemplates a snow bank:

Benediction

Russian Hill
pants don't fit
nothing is a chalice
under my coat

I am thirteen years old
the wind's all wrong
and of course my bald spot
is venerated
as a mirror
a juggler of fourteen hips

Within old-fashioned pieces like this one, meaning is drawn from tangible objects that "arrive remembered." Immigrants whose pants don't fit are inseparable from the child who doubtless knows little about them, but because even that child's voice is submerged in the fourteen hills of San Francisco (hills famous for moving at inopportune times), the hips are both seductive and pernicious. The body, the physical world are constantly threatening the mind of those who are not even aware of how oblivious they are. While an early poem like this one gives the feeling that Vangelisti's poetry was then organized primarily around imagery, it is actually based on an allusion to history, one that is easy to overlook in this single case, but much less so when in the company of the poems that appear in the same volume. And even this point seems trivial unless one reads further into the books that come later— so many serial poems, book-length.

For Vangelisti, ideas do not appear in thin air but must "take place" or be enacted, not just represented in the language of an individual section. *Air's* minutia, ephemera and quotidian detail take on the qualities of air itself: transparent but real, absent and present, often imperceptible but always crucial. To this end, the collage elements of this book are often seamless, conjunctive. The source material takes on slight modifications in syntax and diction to preserve the sense of an experience in which parts and wholes are never entirely separated. This distinguishes the work from some disjunctive modernists who sought to represent the fragmentary nature of their age in a fashion that remained tied to notions of a search or voyage that can't help but lead to father, mother, freedom or Oedipus.

The search in Vangelisti's work always leads away from mental representations to material relationships as they inhabit language. Dialects and particular idioms were adopted, especially those from hard-boiled detective fiction like that of the resolutely West Coast writing of Raymond Chandler or Dashiell Hammett, because they suggest the intellect is no more vital than the body, sensation, the brute force of the signs incarnate. They were idioms of people who did not expect things to cohere reasonably, but to always remain in conflict and in transition. Intellect, rationale come later. At the same time, these idioms emphasize the physical locale, the complexity that can only be captured by the event and not its explication.

With *Portfolio* (originally subtitled "A Novel of Detection"), the event remains physical but the locale is fictional. There is an investigation, though no distinct detective-hero. There is hardly any remnant of the lament Phillip Marlowe occasionally indulged in for a lost order or clear distinctions between good and evil. The very notion of innocence is missing. The collages from sources such as Charles Olson's comments on Melville, in addition to the West Coast detective idioms, serve to implicate everyone, though not perhaps in a crime so much as a community.

Perhaps the culmination of this form is actually the somewhat shorter piece "Gof in Singapore" (*Abandoned Latitudes*, 1983) in which the hero of the poem lacks not only a crime but also a method. What occurs instead is truly detection. The violence is the violence of thought, as signs move from the external world toward the sketchy figuration of the detective-poet. Method is replaced by chance, but here chance is less like that of John Cage and more like that of Pierre Boulez— chance accompanied by constraint. Only under constraint, often very rigorous formal constraint, do the poems signify. The poet-hero is authentic only insofar as he experiences accidental encounters that force him to take on the case, as in "Gof in Singapore," which forces the poet-hero to become also poet-villain: his forgetting that he has prior knowledge of the facts makes him an accomplice.

What is at stake is not consciousness or dreaming but delusion, a public or material hallucination as opposed to a private, pathological one. Thus, the anti-rational disposition is less important ultimately than the interest in sensation, physicality, the actual violence of two bodies in contact, not only the mysteries of language:

> yes
> all it comes to
> she says
> 'cielo e mare'
> sky and sea
> and there are no other questions
> or answers
> no comparisons
> but the thin line her lips are
> in the dark
>> (from "Idiom of Habitation," *The Extravagant Room*, 1976)

And yet this early work seems still too ideological. It starts often from ideas and uses things to prove them. Thus, a method, however truncated, is still there, although what is suggested is perhaps more clear in light of the use of source material such as Olson's *Call Me Ishmael*, Jonathan Edward's sermons or serial murder confessions. Vangelisti is not adopting a tragic element that arguably had been missing in American poetry since William Carlos Williams, rather he is attempting to transform the tragic elements within a literature he is otherwise deeply drawn to. To purge his heroes further of their tragic heritage,

Vangelisti returned to the path begun by the only two modernist American poets he had any real affinity toward: Ezra Pound and T.S. Eliot, particularly their rather anachronistic notions of subjectivity, their refusal to glorify consciousness or present the artist as a dreamer, the art as oppositional dream.

Instead, for Pound and Eliot, art is delirium. Vangelisti's humor, his wackiness is partially misunderstood as "parasurrealism," as Michael Davidson called it in his *The San Francisco Renaissance*. It is the result of an intensely comic journey. Owing a great deal to Vangelisti's "re-education," as he traveled Italy and became ever more clear about the influence of Dante on Eliot and Pound, an influence that, as Giorgio Agamben has shown, was not that of tragic realism, but comic realism.

If comedy is founded on a disjunction between humanity's natural innocence and its personal responsibility, then "making it cohere" might very well be irrelevant, although a movement towards order would remain crucial. The disjunction is ontological, though the art that captures it is conjunctive. In Vangelisti's novels-of-detection, not only is the detective necessarily a villain, not only is society implicated, but the poet's predecessors as well. A cultural history is constantly being recommitted, while the work is gradually less rhetorically committed to its politics. The politics are gradually conveyed more formally. Even the early book *Air* suggests that Vangelisti, at least intuitively, had been working toward this:

Weekend

> gone to the mountains you
> I in the bathtub poem of no heroes
> colder than lukewarm
> slide back days that matter even less
> than the faces between my legs
> float on the phone asking where you are
> until I say it's the cold water
> in the mountains I suppose
> though who can tell people
> been together so long
> the way they begin looking like each
> poem begin looking like that
> the tire two kids roll the phone
> down Sunset Blvd. asking why
> nobody asks what I do in the bathtub
> so long in those mountains
> you are those mountains
> that space out there
> between one word and the next

The poems formal elements show signs of youth: the self-consciousness, the minimal persona used to explore the reader's presence or absence in creating the text. Such celebrations of the surface of the text, the existence of many selves or territories in one person, and the displacement of hierarchies, may appear hopelessly postmodern now. However, the theme of natural innocence as inseparable from collective guilt, the insinuation that such a contradiction is the very ordering principle of subjectivity, are Dantesque. This nascent medievalism, the anachronistic thrust appear more and more clearly in Vangelisti's increasingly sophisticated and less overtly ideological middle period.

All of this to say, the novels-in-verse which follow the early period, particularly *Villa*, *Nemo*, "The Book of Life," and later "Earthly Science," are the result, in part, of Vangelisti's intimate knowledge of the Italian anti-tragic heritage. Drawing on an understanding of medieval culture, he inherits a type of realism that is truly comic, that abandons the notion of mankind as personally and individually innocent while naturally and collectively guilty. In the historical fictions included here, *Villa*, "The Book of Life" and "Gold Mountain," not only is poetic technique drawn from anachronistic devices— bestiaries, alphabet poems, persona, epistolary fiction— but the sort of subjectivity presented is closer to that of Dante's time, especially the way in which a person's interest in expiation is always in conflict with his/her natural innocence.

"Gold Mountain" exemplifies the progress in the development of the novel-in-verse, exploring prostitution and the gold rush from the neglected standpoint of the racist, sexist legacy of Manifest Destiny, as well as from a European perspective. The book is collaged from several 19th and 20th century local sources, and from Van Gogh's letters to his brother Theo, complaining of the role of the artist in a hostile or, at least, indifferent society. Again, the theme in "Gold Mountain" is literally and figuratively one of exile, an historical exile, physical and dispositional, that moves parody beyond parody into an anachronistic futurism, a comic realism.

A book like "The Book of Life," which is indeed based on Dante's trilogy, goes perhaps farther still. The softest, most fluid aspects of what is criticized are also quietly affirmed amid the apparent subversion or appropriation of the original text. Yet, it is a para-parody. It does not merely make a mockery of heaven by emptying it of everyone but 21 divorced women and the journalist/poet. It also cannibalizes the original by using an historical, canonical comedy to reflect on the crisis of the present, its complete obliviousness to such a comic sensibility. Employing Dante's structure, attention is brought to the otherworldly tendencies of art in the first place, its dream of itself as paradise, and the contemporary continuation of this dream. The portrayal is realistic because the dream is based on the almost universal delusion that the point of art is to cheat if not death, then at least anonymity.

The journalistic elements running along the bottom of the pages of

"The Book of Life" bring time into the poem in such a way that newness is cheated altogether. "Gold Mountain" in its own way does this as well. In each case, pathos is achieved, a rare feat in poetry since perhaps that other of Vangelisti's forerunners, Jack Spicer. Like him, Vangelisti uses nearly Oulipean rigor, not simply to happen upon some new formal innovation, but rather as a distinct and particular example of modernist technique, itself an anachronism. As in Spicer's own medieval experiments, the point is to enact voices from history irredeemably lost, except through art. Not the dream of art, but the delusion that art offers us: that our world is best understood by living in another one.

Aesthetically, delusion is different from dream in that it expresses no fantasy of immortality or overcoming of personal weakness, but the reality that art is in our time a game of capturing distinctions. Poetry is a creation of particulars that cannot be appropriated by financial interests and that does not necessarily require maintenance from the critical apparatus of the universities.

At the very least, poetry of this kind is revealed to persist in believing in its importance despite all evidence of its unimportance. Hence, as Gianni Vattimo might say, its weak thought rejuvenates the strong element of humanism which the poetic disciples of Ludwig Wittgenstein cannot abide. "The Book of Life" is, on one level, a critique of poetry's efforts to evade nothingness. It is not a critique of the world but of a virtual world identical in every way to our own. The poet accepts the world as nothing but "the case," though here the Wittgensteinian elements cease. The mocking in "The Book of Life" is not a mocking of how things are, but of the very state of transition those elements are part of, the very same elements the poem also affirms. What is being enacted in the journalistic parts of the work is more like the poem itself coming to accept the absolute mediocrity of its subject, humankind. The indifference to history that Vangelisti personally may despise in the American ethos is simply rendered as a kind of nefarious absent-mindedness, a set of bumbling but violent gestures. The poet himself is never excluded from the embarrassment of survival because survival is the transitional element, the very persistence of the possibility of becoming happy. The mocking is nothing but a movement beyond contempt toward an understanding of humanity as our own joint autobiography. Implied is the political dimension of beauty: that whatever it is, it is never simply disinterested pleasure. And, in a way, Vangelisti's own relative anonymity within the field in which he has long served as translator, editor, publisher, commentator, educator and producer is an advantage. For if "The Book of Life" is written by one who cannot hope to surpass the fame and distinction of the original writer Dante, he nevertheless neutralizes at least one degree of difference. The question that cannot be avoided: how did either book ever actually get written?

If the first was written by a genius— one, by definition, who cannot have been anticipated until the work appears— and the second by someone who would have to be a genius to expect to match the first, then in reality neither book is a work of genius. Genius is the work of history, of cultural forces. The writer's existence is itself only a transitional or preliminary stage, a product of chance, of historical accidents which are constrained to one individual body at more or less one individual moment. The historical forces themselves move on to the work and from the work on to the next accidental vessel, who is sometimes its recipient and who then may follow Vangelisti's lead— to separate the strong element of the old art from the weak element, and find new ways to affirm what strength has been handed down through time.

Hence, anachronistic futurism or comic delirium. What could be more untimely than the bestiary poem, "A Simple Life" (*Alphabets*, 1999), given the almost universal belief that contemporary art must be amoral? Books such as *Villa* or the alphabet poems pose serious questions about the nature of aesthetic judgment, and while they largely remain preliminary investigation, they manage to suggest how an artist may be able to move beyond the post-modern bind of art as non-art without returning to the modernist dogma of art for art's sake. The near-death status of the contemporary poet is surely also a blow to the critical apparatus that reinforces the status of poets like Dante. It is this critical apparatus that has propagated the account of humanity as moving from Edenic order to postmodern chaos, and such apparatus that perpetuates what is essential to tragedy: the starting from order and moving toward chaos, whereas comedy is precisely the opposite movement.

Comedy is not synonymous with parody. It is never simply a resistance to a perceived tradition by way of mock heroics or gestures that may only appear transgressive. Vangelisti reminds us that comedy is necessarily an exploration which gives primacy to existence, not explanation. Included in this is the notion that there can be no existence separated from perception. And while existence must move towards order, even if it is an order of dissipation, it does not have to move towards the order (an apparent chaos) that governs the present. The fragments, the series are an order in themselves: bodies without organs, as Gilles Deleuze might say. Vangelisti helps us see that there is always something human in serious poetry and any effort to expropriate the human is an appropriation of its most crucial element: our sense that there is no community if there is no humanity, no general without particulars.

Vangelisti's is a delirious art, painstaking and rigorous, the sort of delirium one might imagine in the person who first observed that stationary objects are actually made up of moving particles. While the work is full of willful anachronisms, these are anachronisms that have never existed until now.

Standard Schaefer

"It has never been my desire to make sense of painting itself or to argue/defend its practical and social applicability. It's possible that such a viewpoint is marked by unaffected simplicity (a naive sensibility) or outdated romanticism. However, rather than projecting painting (the discipline itself) as majestic, I find it extraordinarily mundane in a very odd way."

— Clarence Morgan

Air
[1970-1973]
1973

ALLEYWAYS

1

those whatever those
the apricot lying on my back are
circling me smaller and smaller
on my lips a fingertip the weight of a song
of those birds of a sun
whatever they are
decree this garden of air

2

not air no not air but what arrives remembered
on the wind sucked in is
deserted of all the brothers fathers lovers
we will never be but foot
beat like gums of old wino crazy in the sun
like Long John curse the dog shit bankers park directors
Coit Tower Fisherman's Wharf St. Peter's and Paul's
steeple even the Pope
waving his three inches of cheese knife at us kids
and the two fat Italian sisters of the poem
bent in half almost pregnant with laughter

3

or Long John feeble in the doorways they say
the alleys is Chinese and the old witch lady
his sister only at night come out of her basement
until the ambulance and she
have a daughter and a husband run off
when his little one go to the Carmelites
who sit forever quiet like sweet birds of prayer
they say

4

those old bald men worth a million in torn sweaters
growing lemons in the fog
smiling at the tourists who say
the chairs tipped back against the basement doors
wine jug in shade
like the Chinese maybe
who never drove a car

5

here I am an immigrant twice over
no bridge repeating secrets in the alleys
nothing here to describe the wind
here every afternoon like the last and final
burning from the East

6

is West of Charlie Parker or
as the French like to put it down
Pas Coeur Pa Cur
mongrel daddy heart without one
for any outside what the song should be
though never be like
living in time too long
in Hollywood where the cars always shine
flowers do not die
people never shout
and the singer must go on
without a song

STYLE

for Jim

of high heels
twirl empty streets
or cloud
plunge into the air
free of words
of suitcases of words
lift a knife how one
slices the window
no shoes but bobby socks
bundles of old woman
like sandbags
scream who enters the glass
and begins to eat

TUNNEL

intestinal 3rd
Street like a telescope backwards
of noon kids no work glistening
dodge along the wall
of mother's teeth promise
too much for any man
this windy day
on foot in Los Angeles
drunk as a nun
and more fragile

YOU

the other one you rhyme
evening inflames
through a cracked window
faucet it hum like rain
woman sometimes
you can hardly speak to
that blind memory
in her eyes
who is there to love
but dream of your own mouth

HOME PLATE

what an Indian summer
a Frisco
crack of the bat
and nothing so ripe
as the statue in your heart

DERBY

that photo
chin way out
cradled in his arms
first hat
is the desperate father
I carry on my back

TAXI

five minutes ago
hit the U-turn hard
olive suit
my grandfather waiting on tables
waving at me
this jangling iron
explodes from the pitcher's hand
real quick even the boss
said he was real quick
the morning how proud
when he spreads out the tips before me
on the kitchen table

swinging open the door the space hot empty space
the flesh abandoned in air
O my song when they have put out your eyes
who will hear you

> QUESTION: DO YOU HAVE A SEXY OUTFIT?
> Rose Walker, *housewife and mother of four:*
> Yes, a one-piece jumpsuit I got at Fredericks.
> Dark blue, it's that new material, the wet look.
> Low cut very tight and sexy looking. It's got a
> hip hugger belt. You wear it with gold heels
> and well...

old beard is dead
the dead are here

> Ethel Crane, *secretary:*
> Let's see, I suppose it's my beige suit with the
> mink collar. I wear a satin shell with it. It's
> quite sexy. How do I know that? You can tell
> by the results you get. I always get good
> results in that outfit.

old beard is dead
the dead are here
turn off the sound
stop the cameras

Alice Soroyan, *sociology professor:*
Just what I'm wearing. It's a kind of a lobster
fisherman's outfit. But seriously I don't wear
deliberately sexy clothes; they're so overpriced.
Sex has become inflated like everything else.
It's out of reach of the common man and, in my
case, the common woman.

old red beard is dead
put the lights out

Mona V. Praeger, *retired Navy secretary:*
Certainly. A blue minidress. I'm 66 and I like to
wear my skirts short. Whenever I have that dress
on they tell me it's sexy and I got beautiful legs.
I used to dance professionally with a little
Italian fellow.

so the barrel must remain behind the ear
begins on the floor of a hot room
the space between the eyes and the rims of the glasses

PARIS – We are told by the Secretary
it is going to be something like signing
travelers checks. By the time he gets to
the 72nd page of the treaty he won't be
able to even recognize his own name.

old red beard is dead
of his own flesh he ate
invisible like air

THE EFFECT OF UNDESIRABLE IMMIGRATION. –
The mental tests given to nearly two million of our soldiers during the last war disclosed large differences in the intellectual ability of various racial groups. Evidence to the same effect is also available from numerous experimental studies. The following conclusions seem warranted.

1. Probably no more than 10 or 15 per cent of American Negroes equal or exceed in intelligence the average White, and the mulatto occupies a position about mid-way between.

jaws even to itself teeth my lips it whistles
to the tune of a mirror
seeing that it's a clear afternoon
and bracelet of cars at the top of Alvarado St.

2. The intelligence of the average American Indian is appreciably but not greatly superior to that of the average Negro. Our Mexican population (Indian hybrids for the most part) which has recently increased with great rapidity, barely surpasses the Negro in average endowment.

3. The immigrants who have been coming to us from the extreme southern and southeastern parts of Europe (South Italians, Portuguese, Greeks and Slavs) are in general distinctly inferior to those who come to us from Northern, Central and Western Europe. The influx of the former has been so great, and their rate of reproduction so excessive, as to give rise to a serious menace.

practically a joke on the whites of my eyes
as if they are eyes
as if they are only words

4. No nation can afford to overlook the danger that the average quality of its germ plasm may gradually deteriorate as a result of unrestricted immigration.

honk the honk of barrio wedding
goddamn plaster every time the door
tailpipe strut on Alvarado north
my one day off
this is Saturday afternoon
or is it or is it

> Vangelisti accomplished the trick with a magic incantation, declaring by fiat that "Marx' most profound commitment was to the primacy of existence over consciousness." This is nonsense. Marx' most profound commitment was to freedom, that is, the ability of human beings, acting through their consciousness, to change the facts of their existence to meet their needs and desires.

cockroach under typewriter
hesitate my fingers
listen to the words
to the voice of the word 'cockroach'
like a face for a woman in another car
tip of my finger stare at what surrounds you
the reader barely possible

> Vangelisti arrives at the ultimate absurdity for a professed admirer of Marx: he reduces "Communism," "Capitalism," "Imperialism," "Progress," "Freedom" to mere "abstractions."

are words I never understand
words I wash from my feet like dirt
words I wash from my forehead like pain

> The madman discovered in a book of China's history that although words like 'benevolence' and 'righteousness' were adorning every page, hidden between the lines were the words 'Ch'ih jen' ('Eat men').... Don't gossip, warned Mayakovsky before his death.

a language of place of words be city of words
of bone and muscle implicit in what sings
around me around it are objects
as other objects have they two faces
poems their own and invisible lick my face
as the wind describes cockroach
on the rim of this glass disturbs the metaphor
creek bottom these my two eyes
and tumble the rest small words
out the infinite hand we have for love

DEADLINE

first the wobbly mattress
three flights up
into abstraction
heaved here sagging
of voice dog-tired
scissors cough like no cymbal
day in day out to objects
of the personal sit
glue pot and headline
ashes ashes
rumor don't fit
in the schoolyard of what was
windy as China
was promised the gust
of a woman in my arms
simply learning to walk

The Extravagant Room
[1975]
1976

and the world which is art
who understands
so much glass
so many windows needed in cars
to entertain the word 'art'
that bread is no commodity
but a hand spread on a wobbly table
a butterfly wearing the saddle
of your own death
and the world which refuses every gesture
not rewritten at the cost of art

•

yet the appetite that we are
a hunger for not remaining alone
reduced to four receding walls
the single perfectly pliable mouth
where all are said to find shelter
to reveal their most peculiar dreams
walking and talking
just like the guy next door

•

and these dreams of
what seems a moment before waking
on one's back
the lines
five or six of them
repeated over and over
like ironing a bright tablecloth
to be remembered
until it is time to remember that one
hardly visible and breathing
in the room

•

though now five or six lines
become twelve ways
of beginning the fantastic
the vacant poem
of becoming what they have become

    •

one foot in the dark
tracing the cool grain of the floor
the dog is asleep
the children are asleep
flower pots at the open window
crouching like three cats
each minute or so
a woman somewhere cackles
what must have once been a laugh
though little matters
but the sheet caught between your knees
as you lie here asleep
fingers tracing on your hips
the same thing my foot is thinking
there is no metaphor for this sheet
this distance drawing me

    •

so awkward this 'drawing'
maybe that is the value
a resilience to even extravagant use
like the old joke about the fastest draw in the West
like the old joke about the fastest draw in the West
like the old joke about the fastest draw in the West

    •

to say nothing of
the puckered heart
painted on tit or forearm
the flirtation of conscience
we offer the earth
the very air we run through our fingers
as if it were a gift

•

because he is asking to sit down
actually at the same table sit down
when there are ten other tables
wearing a suit without a tie
the accent of small business
empty rooms and children
slaughtered in a century beyond dreams
a history which has stopped
begun again and stopped
though he repeats his question
and adds if I don't mind

•

to say nothing
of what some chose not to say
denying the beast
the light-guzzling aperture
of that dreamy performance
we have all been promised from birth

•

good night good night
as in New York New York
that time of night
not hard to imagine Land's End
the ocean the rocks below
oblivious and fresh
as that first morning you woke up
next to her

•

nudging as if knees and feet
under the table
to end here
to begin once more
that face
that clarity of lost heroes
in search of a delirious afternoon
hoping for a phone call
to break off this poem

    •

not even shadows of what little we dare
but the suggestion
of dreadful odds and ends
some voice not quite overheard
a matchbook in your pocket
from a city you have never been
an odor the back of a hand
which is no one else's but hers
who is not here

    •

so the terror of innocence
the telephone calls continuing
to wake in a cold sweat
or maybe just the hopelessness
of certain poems
small ecstasies evoked
and as quickly forgotten
all but the sequence of syllables
the conclusion of an argument
like the color of someone's eyes
you simply cannot remember

    •

of police and helicopters
the drone hammerlike
the hunger that is waking
words which are not words
but more like persons voices
missing in a place
one may never trust

•

and the language which is art
what is it so different
making new readers
of new poems
or as a painter said it once
working all night
into the first glance of morning
the room is so large
each corner and nick on the floor
as if the eyes are coming
right out of your head

•

yet the pronoun
the I of this peculiar vision
prone to sense what is not stated
to state what is not prone to sense
the sympathy of color after light rain
the size of windows and parked cars
the boundaries of this and every other afternoon
the telephone poles
the pencil
the light switches
growing so small
one is left holding nothing
but one's breath

•

something like naming vision
though by naming vision
it is more improbable
less complex
than the vertical ambition
of naming love
in our own likeness

•

and 'likeness'
the bath the heat of water
as we lay back hardly touching
and likeness
the word unwanted
not understood
the likeness of what is not love

•

there are islands
moments of rock and coral
where ships vanish
because they are parables
and there is no communication out there
but the reconstruction of whimsy
chance encounters
phrases one can't finally remember
and there is a quiet about the eyes
almost green this quiet
and sometimes even green the eyes

•

without an answer
November brought you
from the east the wind shakes the houses
the warm mornings
the livid afternoons
knives and forks salt shakers even
glowing enormous with the size of it
to shipwreck
to discover an island
to cross out so many words
you can recite them even in your dreams

•

yes
all it comes to
she says
'cielo e mare'
sky and sea
and there are no other questions
or answers
no comparisons
but the thin line her lips are
in the dark

•

simple as picking or
not picking up a pencil
not only the telling of it
is what brings one to the page
but the preoccupation
with what continues unspoken
as a man walking his bicycle
turns his head
at the passing windows

•

so the terror of innocence
a justification of marble eyes
which are not marble
but the color of a sparrow's beak
stiff and upside down
when it dies
the little wire legs
like a TV antenna
like that stuttered pronoun I I

•

sea and sky
which is not art
anymore than they are its inspiration
which is only the impossible fact
of not dreaming
what we are

•

We are on the other side of a window in a room which expands and retracts. The room is there because we have never been. It is furnished with the sound of two people talking into the night though the sun has already been up for a few hours. It is winter and the streams are low and translucent as August. The eucalyptus are dry and noisy though by the color of the hillside it must have rained yesterday. The two are listening. They have stopped talking but are not aware of having done so.

Portfolio
[1975-1976]
1978

though it does not seem a problem
the identity of the dream or dreamer
whether the faceless hand twisting the doorknob
is your hand
or whether it is your hand
or whether it is the faceless hand

Event 7: Big Apple

But tonight you have nothing to fear, he has taken it into his head to be serious. The film begins with a wonderful dolly shot across the outdoor and indoor splendors of Versailles. Obviously there isn't a word of truth in the preceding tale—he is the best behaved little boy in Paris. Until we arrive at, in one of the great halls, a man in Sun King apparel with his back to us talking—but to whom? these windows? the pale motionless curtains? the footsteps? the stars below in the street? So let us return to pleasure, which promises to overtake you and, with two little notes of music, win you over to the idea of skin, and many other ideas as well. But the pangs of the artist are lacerating, even couched in minutiae. Concerning a cigarette commercial, Henri worries intensely whether it was artistically right to have done it with gloves on. Even if there's nothing up the sleeve but two dead men named earth and fire and uncle. During the dubbing of an animal cartoon, Pierre, who does one of the silly animal voices, complains that the line 'idiot turtle' doesn't feel right. About bigger problems one kids oneself because it's not losing count that's bitter but flying off to sleep with a whole suburb of newspaper stuck in the throat.

Event 8: L'Enfant Terrible

And the voice continuing without hands or feet arms or legs teeth hair even a nickname. But it's also something deeper and more moving: the fact that even those who fail at both art and life, who play badly in both domains, believe in, suffer for, and truly live only in their restless playacting. Where there is no music as a child but the sound of committing memory to names and dates and holidays. The first time he killed himself was to annoy his mistress. That virtuous creature brusquely refused to sleep with him, saying she was overcome by remorse for her faithful lover of no music as a child but the sound of knives and forks in the throat the sensation around the neck. So the problem, a profoundly human one, is *volupté*, for which there is, alas, no proper English equivalent. No stopping it without a nickname without music only the sound of plates on which the future is served.

Event 9:

From the sublime to the ridiculous. But then you might believe what he tells you, you might even say you like it surrounding you like a millionaire fitting his lips to a Cuban cigar. The story is partly trivial, partly unbelievable. The people are too bad, too good or too stupid to be true, and neither plot nor dialogue comes to the rescue. Yes, it don't flush right and nobody will take the time to take the top off it because it's always full up to here with talk. As if there was a tomorrow, as if what this contrived and banal film elicits is a sense of regret. Traditionally, however, sculpture has been involved with getting it up—with moving stone, wood or metal masses off the earth onto a base (i.e. to eye level), and from the base farther upward, into the sky. Though he wakes slowly this morning his mind is very clear. He is your prisoner you are his. His doubts have materialized, his negations are made flesh. He lives what he once imagined himself living: at last he has found himself a disciple. He licks his forefinger and raises it in the air.

Event 10: the Wave

As it continues at 19 a dropout from his second year of junior college, he manages to enlist in a local Coast Guard unit. A few months earlier he had begun to write poetry and experiment with the derangement of his senses. In freshman philosophy there is a likeable creature with only two dimensions. 'Now consider', says the professor, 'consider this animal creeping across a sphere; what does it see?' At age 17 we are watching him and his girl friend on a local quiz program. The program host is asking him what his ambitions are after high school. Our hero grins broadly and answers. 'One has always suspected that the creature doesn't see anything, it feel—it's an ultimate connoisseur of surfaces.' He remembers at 7 years old when he became quite good at telling time asking his father why they kept the clock five minutes fast. Then when he was 11 it was set ten minutes ahead, when he was 14 fifteen minutes ahead and now, shortly after his 16th birthday, the clock is running twenty minutes fast. For even stylization can't explain why a regulator known to be such should pretend to be crazy birdwatcher—unless he really is crazy, in which case, how could he be so very nearly invincible? Little is reproduced of his childhood. The few vivid memories relate to comic books, dinosaurs, National Geographic and countless hours with adults who always seem to be asking him questions. Readers of this column will know by now that its writer believes in film as art, and in art as a form of humanism. He again becomes his position on the crest of the wave. We re-examine the frozen action: excellent form, an apparent confidence in his smile and the wave, the amazing perfection of the wave.

Event 11: Lost Angels

Magnetic violin and the words desert him. In the air terminal the 60s continue to be replayed. The long hair, the knapsacks, the guitar picked with three fingers on a pane of glass. Spread before you are the Sunday classifieds bought a day early to get a jump on other brokers. New listings are to be circled in red. Attain the most passive or receptive state of mind. Forget your genius, your talents, those of everyone else. What remains we hazard in a phrase, an oblique scorn for the boundaries white of the sheet before us. Known for your long blond hair and unconventional wardrobe—hot-pants for lunch at the Bistro, for instance—you have been in the business for 19 years, save a three year hiatus during your show-biz marriage. 'Anybody who doesn't make big money in real estate today has got to be an idiot,' you observe. 'In fact, even the idiots are making money.' Now come to the end of it, 30 hands without a gesture, 12 ribs without a single sun, only the one extravagance, a low angel shot of stampeding cattle. 'You fight hard to maintain your feminine identity. Some of the women get so hard and competitive. In real estate it's just a matter of who gets there first, since we all have the same clients.' Said the generals: to camouflage, vanish, amalgamate with the earth, to make a life for ourselves of branches never yellowing.

Event 12

It's not far, as the crow flies, from cloud to man. There are, broadly speaking, two kinds of artistic greatness: that of transcending previous boundaries, of defying all norms and conventions; and that of perfect taste, of working exquisitely within one's limits. A mouth around which the world turns. Though we were involved in civil rights, in the peace movement, in Cuba, for us the single most revolutionary change that has come out of the 60s has been in personal relationships. Let's not perfect or embellish what is opposed to us. When the divorce becomes final, the wife will not be able to meet the mortgage payments. That's what we call a motivated seller. In fact, Vasari relates that Piero di Cosimo would at times remain plunged in contemplation of a wall on which sick people customarily spat; from the spots he formed equestrian battles, the most fantastic cities and the most magnificent landscapes ever seen; he did the same with clouds in the sky. At this point a tap on the shoulder, a pair of gray eyes excuse themselves asking if we've arrived at a definition of language yet, especially the part about hubcaps and popcorn or aren't we scheduled to make a stop there at all.

Event 13:

Few dreams and even those become precarious, uncontrollably banal like the sets of teeth near your elbow on the bus. Because even among themselves they are strangers; crossing the mountains at every bend in the river it is obvious why no one stops there. Spared by bores and boredom one may find suicide the accomplishment of the most unselfish gesture provided that one is not curious about death. The French word means bliss, ecstasy, sexual fulfillment: it suggests a slow, protracted, intense and sensual delight, for which 'pleasure', the customary translation, is much too weak. For this they will beat up a drunk and toss him in the river for dead. The day is coming when to touch something, to get acquainted, one will strangle a woman, shoot her in her sleep, open her head with a hammer. [Editor's note: Jacques Rigaut killed himself with a revolver on November 5, 1929.] So listen to the door remove the wind, to the door speak through the grass like cat's eyes.

Event 14:

The ultimate consequence, the receipt of water, bears no useful or mechanical relation to the form of the behavior of 'asking for water'. Indeed, it is characteristic of such behavior that it is impotent against the physical world. 'I know how Custer felt,' one school official sighed, 'I've never seen so many Indians.' District officials now require teachers who claim to be Indians to present a letter from the chief of their tribe. And so on until he wakes to dream doing it for the sport, for the international spirit of cooperation of her as she is dry sport. In fact, if the eyes of a lover were a million stars, Plato was fond of saying. But in the case of a proper noun a difficulty remains. Assuming there is only one man named Doe, is Doe himself the meaning of Doe? Even among the white middleclass there is a remarkable problem of classification. Besides the hip professional and the professionally hip, one will encounter such diverse types as university professors, gay militants, Russian refugees, art activists and just plain eccentrics, like the lady on Avon Park Terrace who collected 187 mason jars of urine before she was carted away. Critics have everywhere remarked on the agricultural nature of much of American literature, particularly that of the 18th, 19th and early 20th centuries. And lick and grind slowly the spirit certainly the team spirit that continues to be written the time. Certainly the team points doubling the sport of each mount and dismount, from point of waking to port of entry to the international publicity of a team nature. So Hughes had ordered his plane to fly up to San Francisco, found out from the hotel where he could locate the chef, sent a car to fetch him, flew him back down here and had him cook crepe suzette for us. Now if that doesn't impress a girl I don't know what does. Ascending the spiral within the chamber, within the ear of waking her mounting time dismounting her waking.

Event 15: Photo

Is his creativity out of focus? What's missing from these pictures? He understands the basis of photography, his equipment is good and his enthusiasm is boundless. Still there may be a missing factor which prevents his pictures from standing out in a crowd. Or to put it another way, what is there of a dog Jack doing in this poem? One had lost heart simply because a rabbit hardly seemed a worthwhile subject and so one feels a certain self-satisfaction at having persisted in the effort. Or e.g., black Jacques becomes Jack in his son's mouth, slightly larger than the breed's average, given to the skinning of teeth out of excitement or disgrace. It really seems that one's technique has become automatic, so that without deliberately thinking of it, one's ideas come out in the form of images, as in obedience to some fanciful law. Or e.g., grinning tumbleweed descending a staircase darkly. And one is very much afraid it is time to change the tune, or at least the instrument. Or e.g., still-life of freshly made bed with black shaggy cloud feigning sleep.

Event 16: Aphrodite

Simply knowing what it is moves between us like skin glows around a glass of water. So we continue by developing the related image of skin—smell = sexual potency—seen by one of the men who identifies himself with smooth skin, has no smell and sees himself resembling the teenage boy who has legs like a snake and is still waiting to pass the test of love. Of islands which somehow lack metaphor which prohibit such isolated words where all is excusable as it can be argued that the poem, concerned with disillusionment, began in the first person plural with the adjectives in the masculine; the idea of using as a protagonist a prostitute who takes up her former life probably came later, and then the adjectives become feminine and the poem develops the theme of the prostitute; an effort is made to put everything in the third person; then it returns to the third person plural with the adjectives in the masculine and eliminates the more explicit references to the prostitute's life in such a way that—in spite of the title—it seems the poet is speaking of himself. In fact he made the imprudent gesture of speaking of his admiration, maybe even used the term affection, for a poet the others considered nothing short of 'political'. The others pointedly ignoring his remark, taking a few hits off a joint, sipping their beers and disputing who among them had written the fewest poems in the last two years. Valentine's Day the day before tomorrow, all of them obliging desires unlikely as their names. And her husband tells her that her lover is becoming passive and she reminds her lover that he should at least get some ideas down on paper and the lover's wife proclaims this the year of material possessions and he, the lover, makes a joke no one laughs at, not even the four year-old girl with whom he is being sarcastic.

Event 17: Badger

Ground-up beetles and rhinoceros horn, bull's testicles and ginseng—all were tested and found lacking. Because this man is not a mere psychopath but a walking textbook of perverted crime: sex maniac, sadist, rapist, vampire, strangler, hammer-killer, arsonist, a man who commits bestiality and achieves orgasm witnessing street accidents. Though if he could only read in that country's sky north and south, pronounce her name without the small agony of names. On Taiwan the dawn comes up like thunder behind Badger's new chemical processing plant. A bird's voice, a piping frog enlivens the solitude. In fact, the sun rarely sets on Badger because Badger is where it all comes together, like the extreme blue of a postcard sky, Badger doesn't just mean striking hard bargains Yankee style but getting away from the crush of civilization, the enfeeblements of culture. So when dietary indiscretions are removed, performance and pleasure are found to increase, which can only lead to the conclusion that good food is the best aphrodisiac. Subsequently, Emerson reports endless seeking with no past at his back, while, after considerable testing, Whitman discovers no sweeter meat than sticks to his bones. Space remains the dominant presence, the most urgent metaphor of the American imagination: a sacred emptiness of space, an ecstasy of the essential man, free of social bonds, in deep relation with the tangible world. Maybe he can remember the word for 'cricket' she made him repeat, how like a chirrup it sounded, so many consonants on the lip.

Event 18: Paree

In the few moments before that walk and the blow that will separate his head from his body, he has already expressed his last earthly desire. This provides the long, useful writer's retrospective so easily enriched by the passage of time as it begins to shorten itself on paper and take its shadow from a pen dipped in ink. Where teeth grow numb growing words below the waist of the simplest words, even those one might have for love. Then he asks the prison doctor if, after one's head has been chopped off, one is still able to hear, at least for an instant, the sound of one's own blood gushing from the wound. Savoring the thought he adds that this would of course be the pleasure to end all pleasures. Even those of a poetry cynical as the corpse of ambition, the pun applied for the sake of pure science, linking penthouse to poontang, senate to firing squad. Since the lavishing of such heroic tact in the lining of such rough and ostensibly arbitrary forms seemed stunningly perverse at the time, and many people, this writer include, still don't quite know what to make of it. Most observers believe it is too early to tell what, if any, effects the federally funded program will have on the nation's arts or if we managed to save any artists of potential importance from drifting off into other professions. In spite of appalling crimes, he is far from the maniac of conventional films. He is no Count Dracula with snarling teeth, no lumbering stitched-together Frankenstein monster. What one really misses most is the voluptuous writing about nature with which she was so impetuously and watchfully in love, writing which is necessarily absent here—descriptions of fleshy fruit buds and sharp green leaves, of willow sprouts as yellow as hair, of colors and odors in spring or autumn hedgerows. There is no sign of the brutal sadist or the weak-lipped degenerate. All praise of animate, speechless vegetal nature in fields and forests has been omitted from this book, whose concern is human passion and physical sexual love, which are customarily practiced indoors. With sleek, meticulously parted hair, cloud of Eau de Cologne, immaculate suit and well-polished shoes, he looks like a prim shopkeeper or minor civil servant. So as the word 'pure' falls from his lips, one hears the trembling of the plaintive 'u', the icy limpidity of the 'r' and the sound arouses nothing in one but the need to hear again its unique resonance, its echo of a drop that trickles out, breaks off and falls somewhere with a plash. In the nostrils in the throat the slow chest, in the blaze rapid as a candle aglow with the pump of it, hissing the backbone, the uncoiled intestine of dreams that we are.

Event 19: Rembrandt

A week now that ragged black dog nuzzling the curb 400 miles north of here as if it were asleep. So we begin with an extensive appreciation of a woman called 'Charlotte', a generous cocotte who stimulates long, nightingale-like cries of satisfied love because they give felicity and triumph to her dying young lover. As one drowsier with the wind whipping elm and cypress, the odor of last night's fire, a sky so blue the bottom looks fallen out. The elder of the two gentlewomen keeps a diary of continuous small joys, referring to her companions in terms such as 'my Love' or 'my Delight': 'Read Mme. deSevigne. My Love drawing'. Or: 'At ten my Beloved and I drank a dish of tea. A day most delicious and exquisite in its refinement.' Filled with information about people, companies, charitable organizations and churches, government bodies and absolutely amazing places that need quick wit and literacy to write on countless subjects. Or: 'Sweet sunshine, blue sky, birds innumerable. My beloved and I went a delicious walk round Edward Evans' field.' Since most of it is done evenings and weekends, sitting cross-legged in front of the typewriter, on a richly luxurious carpet in a penthouse with an incredible skyline view. Sir Walter Scott and other distinguished travelers finally begin calling on them, for the grace of their elegant manners and concentrated tenderness. Because brain-boggling as it might seem, there is a real shortage in this world of people who can write the English language without stubbing their toe on a comma. Think about this for a moment, then read the following. Rembrandt etched THE THREE TREES during a time when he was preoccupied with light and swirling action. While the principal motif is a group of trees, touched with highlights and shadows, their massed foliage interpenetrating, the etching is alive with sunshine and storm, and with wind that sends clouds flying. Now look at this etching again. Fire and flood sweep the world. Sinister hybrids break into every bedroom, electric paperweights play comfortable in well-known Parisian archways, lion-headed men go undeterred to the guillotine, a commodious railway carriage makes its last stop half-way up the Sphinx. Now look at the etching again. A vision, that is to say a device of snouts and raw fish, clogged gutters and cabbages, wet streets in an unfamiliar city, mirrors that won't come clean, twilight, tiny spoons of coffee stirring all day long. Now look at the etching again. This classic makes its statement more strongly than ever, with a contemporary cut, attention to detail and the particular uniqueness of its fabric. Now look at the etching once more. Do you see more in it now? Feel greater involvement? If you do, you already see more, feel more, know more about Rembrandt—and about art.

Event 20: the Whale

Narrative of the Most Extraordinary and Distressing Shipwreck of the Whaleship Essex, of Nantucket; Which Was Attacked & Finally Destroyed by a Large Spermaceti-Whale in the Pacific Ocean. And why it s a place where no one looks at faces, which is to say flesh, as inviolate as the ripe sunset our hero rides off into. To begin he took space to be the central fact to man born in America. Plus a harshness we still perpetuate, a sun like a tomahawk, small earthquakes but big tornadoes and hurricanes, a river north and south in the middle of the land running out the blood. A subsequent visit to her upstairs neighbor to complain about the noise leads to the idea of photographing all the living rooms in the building. To expedite the project she sends a form letter explaining that she is doing a photo essay 'to show how we use the space around us to reflect ourselves'. Big? Melville may never have seen the biggest of the whales, the blue, 100 feet, at 11 years, lives 20 to 25 years, and weighs 150 tons—or four times the estimated weight of the biggest prehistoric monster and equal to the weight of 37 elephants or 150 fat oxen. Yes and one might add it began in silence, though more the sympathy of a morning suitable to the skin, no metaphors or meaningful glances insisting where we go from here. At this point the prosecution raises a strong objection. He says he has listened to so many big words and foreign words are being used here, and the constitution expressly provides that trials must be conducted in the English language. Yes, the year Moby Dick was being finished Marx was writing letters to the NY Daily Tribune. Typical of mail is a note from a man recently divorced after a 30 year marriage. He was always suspicious about his wife but he had only a second grade education and, as he puts it, was still pretty dumb then. He didn't begin to add things up until after she had two children who, he claims, can't possibly be his. Even so, he says he has always been a good father to them and they have never had any idea they are illegitimate. In fact, in Shakespeare's tomb lies infinitely more than Shakespeare ever wrote. For in this world of lies, truth is forced to fly like a white doe in the woodlands. Thus the question: he is making out his will and has brothers and sisters who could really use the money. He owns his home plus some stocks and savings and doesn't see why he should leave anything to his illegitimate children. And finally, he asks, who should be punished?

Event 21: the Whale (cont.)

And at age 33 she comes to the capitol walking among its buildings, gardens, even windows vaster and more imposing than she has words for and after three days of almost complete silence she wakes and begins speaking to her son in a language the citizens of that capitol call 'poetry'. The American whaling industry—in contrast to the Basque, French, Dutch and English—develops independently, concentrates on different species of whale, covers all seas including the arctic and yields on a larger scale than in any other country or group of countries. The notebooks reveal that meticulous accounts of daily expenses are kept. They also show that replies to his matrimonial advertisements have been carefully classified and information has been filed about their fortunes, children, relations and so on. The names are briefly marked under the following headings: 1) To be answered poste restante. 2) Without money. 3) Without furniture. 4) No reply. 5) To be answered to initial poste restante. 6) Possible fortune. 7) To be further investigated. More than any contemporary politician, he is a self-made man—a creation raised up out of nowhere by his own wit, will and unremitting concentration. He possesses a lively and wide-ranging intelligence: in more relaxed circumstances, he listens to Wagner and Bob Dylan, reads a novel or blueprint with equal absorption and forces Xerox copies of the poetry of Dylan Thomas on his friends, In flight Los Angeles to San Francisco the very young and the very old continue looking down. The rest scanning vinyl-bound magazines and reports, the 'suchness' of progress, the pure habits of investment, the sound of light in the sound of pages turned, lips puckering to sip the vodka, the icy cigarette. Perhaps if he had not been asked to narrate and compose music for television documentary about adopted children in search of their natural parents, he would never have begun his own search wobbling down the tracks with a picnic basket and selling them at a nickel a bag. Later, he and an older cousin go into partnership collecting old newspapers and scrap iron and hawking refreshments to the farmers when they come to town on Saturdays. Obviously there is a need for people to participate actively and personally in art forms rather than be removed observers. In wearing a piece of art, in touching or using it in any way, one is allowing other persons to make closer connections with art, to participate in the rituals these creations suggest. Who would eat his own flesh in this climate, an appetite large as the heat itself, the low buildings yellow and lavender and white, who would speak to you as if he knew you were dying. At age 9 he gambled on five bales of cotton at a depressed 5 cents a pound, sold it later at 18 cents, bought five tenant shacks—and rented them for years to the local poor at an aggregate $16.50 a month. He had the tradition in him, deep, in his brain, his words, the salt beat of his blood. He had the sea of himself in a vigorous, stricken way and, like most Americans, one aim: lordship over nature. In fact, as it is told in local lore, it was his mother who gentled him—who encouraged him in his schoolwork, routed him out of bed for church and infected him with that sense of unease of the privileged called social conscience. So here or 'present' as one was called upon to repeat, raising a hand up high the first day of school twenty-five years ago.

Event 22: the Whale (cont.)

The development of means of transportation, of various forms of international life and tourism favors mobility, travel and meetings. But the number of and rapidity with which contacts are being established may obliterate cognitive sensitivity and absorptive ability. In fact, for all the parallels between best-seller lists and library-reading tastes, regional variations do occur. For example, local pride probably explains the popularity of 'The Dukes of Durham' at the Durham, N.C. public library, and even 'Polygamist's Wife' in Salt Lake City, Utah. Some local favorites remain inscrutable, such as the popularity of 'Police Training in the U.S.' and 'The Companion Guide to London' at the Montgomery, Ala. Public library. In no language a sure idiom for leaving, the gist of it refining words to numbers on a dial, ash blown furiously off the sleeve. Maybe the gestures come closer, an embrace, the wave of a hand repetitive as the dawn that will not come again. Because he smells Los Angeles before he gets to it. It smells stale and old like a living room that has been closed too long. But the colored lights fool one. The lights are wonderful. There ought to be a monument to whoever invented neon lights. Fifteen stories high, solid marble. There's a man who really made something out of nothing. As they chant Attica and Cia, continuing to drown him out, he holds out an upturned fist then extends his middle finger and gives a sharp stab upward. Asked whether this is dignified behavior for the Vice-President of the United States, he replies, 'It isn't very dignified of them, frankly, to give the finger to the Vice-President of the United States.; Yet he also understands that the American dreamer, for all his odysseys and exiles, for all his tired knowledge, cannot give up on the American dream even if the dream gives upon him. To play a skeptic cursed with hope is the role he will comically and heroically be stuck with until the last camera blinks off. It is this type of contact, which lives in our memory, that our editorial board has in mind when announcing our new competition, entitled 'My Meeting With a Pole'. (This is meant to include a meeting with a woman, a man, a child or group of people.) The bug wobbles a little as it crosses the desk, like an old woman carrying too many parcels. At another desk a nameless detective keeps talking into an old-fashioned hushaphone mouth-piece, so that his voice sounds like someone whispering in a tunnel. Asked how he would do it over again, he says wealth wouldn't be his primary objective—progress and advancement would. If he could afford schooling, he'd pursue one of three careers: engineering, science or law. He thinks he'd get as much schooling as possible. But not too much—there is such a thing as overdoing it. The detective talks wit h his eyes half-closed, a big scarred hand on the desk in front of him holding a burning cigarette between the knuckles of the first and second fingers. The bug reaches the end of the desk and marches straight off into the air. Because even the gestures are noth ing but approximate as if tossing pebbles into a well or dozing through pine and sloping pastureland more than half-a-day beyond the Polish border, taking some comfort that here are no monuments to poets and the train keeps moving very fast.

Event 23: Post-Operative

One might fancy calling 'sheep-backed' these dark straggling clouds but it is almost New Years, the dusk more meager than night here at the desert's edge. And these transfigurations of bars and stripes on the back or maybe the belly of a creature so vast is only partially seen. If you read an appliance instruction book, an auto repair manual, the tags on a new dress or suit, a menu, a tax form, a catalog, a recipe, a department store ad, a cartoon, a record jacket, a book blurb, you are reading the work someone else has been paid to write. For example, Georgette Lieberman, a composer and Time magazine proofreader, pictured here on her snake sofa with German shepherd, Kyrie, took this apartment for the dropped living room and what she calls the 'bay windows'. In fact, she even remembers a Sunday service in her blue period when the preacher asked the communicants whether, if they were arrested for being Christians, there would be evidence enough to convict. She took the question personally and decided the answer was no. Lieberman adds that the people who previously lived in the apartment meditated in the living room and she too feels it is a 'very peaceful room'. So she has made it a place to read and relax in and keeps nothing in the room to remind her of her daily occupation. If you listen to a newscast, a TV situation comedy, a lecture, a taped supermarket sales pitch, a business presentation, a fund-raising appeal, a sermon, you are listening to words you might have put down on paper yourself. And what he writes to her from the coast of Sicily though the scirocco abated the torso of this same creature muffles the air. But then he is listening to a moon tossed along the waves to the withdrawal of a language terrible as what crowds this night. As husband and wife, they are living, as well as teaching, the techniques of super-marriage—the joyful relationship every husband and wife may achieve. Now they draw upon professional and personal experience to help one another discover and possess sexual loving that goes beyond marriage vows to complete psychosexual union. Of course it is stone that meets our frustration as stone itself is met by the color of the sea or as the saying goes in West Africa somewhere is a place where the grass meets the sky and that place is called the end. What happens when one is invited to appear on a TV talk show? What goes on behind the scenes at one of those glittering literary cocktail parties? How can you survive your first four-martini lunch with a publisher? How do other celebrities survive grueling promotion tours? How can you get bigger and better fees on the lecture circuit? How can you get more satisfaction out of success? How can you help your family and friends accept your super-stardom? And because society leaves nearly all of us with some sexual inhibitions, the Sterns have devised effective techniques for strengthening all areas of sexual loving: a communication game called 'Tennis Match' in which both players must either win or lose; a secret ritual that can excite the most inhibited of women; a technique of non-demand sex which adds daily joy and fulfillment to tired marriages; a way in which sexual fantasies can restore excitement to too-familiar sexual patterns. 'Choosing furniture for one's home,' says psychiatrist Dr. Donald Green, 'is an area of mutuality and cooperation.' 'We have uncannily similar tastes,' says psychologist Dr. Susan Zimmerman. Dr. Green brought back the carved wooden furniture in the living room from El Salvador when he served there in the Peace Corps. Other Central American objects were acquired on a recent trip together. Because turning from her face those lights on the trolley bouncing on and off as she demands how time has been or may be to them as she claims they have not spoken when all they have left is speech. The couple keeps books in every room. Although Dr. Green likes to read his journals while listening to music in the living room, the books stored there are definitely more recreational. One reason for his has been generally recognized. Stage performances merely transposed, rather than translated to the screen become too broad, brash, big for the film medium, which quite literally magnifies gestures and expressions. For example , Jill Salerno, an independent producer of TV commercials, took the apartment for the Southern exposure and the 'clear view for five blocks'. But a less noted reason may be even more important: a screen adaptation falls, precisely, flat—a limited but three-dimensional space sprawls into an unlimited but two-dimensional one. In fact, she and singer/songwriter/guitarist Sheldon Perkins use the sunken living room for music and entertainment. Jill claims proudly that there is nothing in the room from Bloomingdale's and that she has never actually been tempted to buy anything new. Now, farce, especially the kind that depends on a multiplicity of doors flying open and shut as ill-sorted people rush through them toward outrageous consequences, needs the stage space to play with. They used to have the couch facing the mirrors, but people couldn't stand facing themselves so they turned them around. The TV is in the bedroom because, as Jill puts it, she doesn't like to watch TV with company. 'It's crude,' adds Sheldon. The best thing, however, is an opening close-up of an egg yolk slithering through an hourglass. It is impossible to say whether it is an old Italian custom at death vigils, a proleptic reference to what the film will wind up with all over its face or a piece of pure surrealism like Dali's melting watches. For example, freelance photographer Barbara Pepper rents the apartment because of its European feeling and because it accommodates her concert grand piano. Her space isn't planned, however, and she adds that very little has been bought purposefully. In short, take away the spatial antics of farce, its solid geometry, and one is left with little more than a flimsy contrivance. The Oriental rug is a gift from her mother and most everything else has been gathered in her travels. The mirror is from Mexico, the coffee grinder a gift from a Bedouin in Israel. But recently her apartment has become less crowded, an expression of something new. As she says, she has a longing for a great deal more space. Where there is smoke there might have been promises or maybe it's only the coastline here in California that is so much like Sicily and the resolutions made north of both.

Lately, however, there is only watching grandfather, the predictable and helpless scenarios of life with the old man. Grandfather having trouble with stairway grandfather dizzy rising from dinner grandfather sleeping later and later. For example, Las Vegas police report that a man calling himself John the Baptist may be responsible for four fire bombings of area churches within the last two weeks. The man, telephoning a local newspaper, takes full responsibility for the fires and vows to continue burning the city's churches. On the other hand, the best living American novelist is also a man of brains. Seasoned reader, veteran talker, he handles ideas with the same juggling ease that he tells stories. Not given to thinking small, he recently urged both the third world and the industrial rich to put aside petty grievances over narrow issues and concentrate on nothing less than a global compact to eradicate poverty by the end of the 20th century. In fact, the reporter who took the call claims that the Baptist sounds very serious and is adamant about getting his message printed in the newspapers. Steeped in the mysticism of Chicago but still responsive to the war cries of ideology, this great writer also proves to be a great listener. Like every other visitor of Israel, he soon tumbles into a gale of conversation. He loves it: it makes him feel at home. But don't think whaling different from any other American industry. The first men in it are workers. The money and the glory come later, on top with the exploiters. And the force goes down, stays where it stays where it always does, at he bottom. So very little is said about the dreams themselves, traces of childhood where events revolve in the most gratifying and terrible of orbits where questions are carefully asked of bystanders who look like none of the family. Then as now the trick remains to reduce labor costs lower than the worker's efficiency—during the 1840s and 1850s it cost the owners 15 cents to 30 cents a day to feed each crew member—and combine inefficient workers and such costs by maintain the lowest wages and miserable working conditions. Of course, one tries to be representative, the selector says, including poets who are established in a more steady way—who have a body of work and have embarked on a direction that's profitable and not a dead end. The result is that by the 1840s the crews on the whale-ships are the bottom dogs of all nations and all races. Of the 18,000 men, one-half ranked as green hands and more than two-thirds deserted every voyage. One mistrusts oneself as much as one endorses oneself, says the selector. While one moves among one's biases as consciously as possible, the primary test, though , must remain the intrinsic merit of the poem. Oddly, enough, Americans still fancy themselves such democrats. But their triumphs are of the machine. It is the only master of space the average person ever knows, ox-wheel to piston, muscle to jet. It gives trajectory. In fact, even with her it is hard to talk about dreams of grandfather, a man eighty years-old and in perfect health. She simply replies that the man must be at least about eighty and, after all, what does anyone expect. Finally a try at changing the subject, claiming how death surrounds them in that place, the Porsche in the rearview mirror all the way to work, the immobility the strange comfort found easing into bed late when she is already asleep.

Event 25: Work

Shaking her head if there is no more to it than apricot as it sags with fruit but surely some hope some pleasure is in being here under the sun. Consider, for example, this mechanical bank. To load, simply draw back gun sight, lay coin flat on top of gun barrel. Hide bear by pushing his head down into tree trunk. Lower green leaves over tree trunk. His intentions towards her are entirely dishonorable which is to say vital in comparison to that circle of petty literary virtues where all gets leveled to the talk of old men and women speculating on the regularity of their bowels, In the middle ages the laws of the church guaranteed the laborer ninety rest days, fifty-two Sundays and thirty eight holidays, during which he was strictly forbidden to work. This, for the Protestant, is the great sin of Catholicism. In fact, writers open up in these pages because they are talking to colleagues and interested, intelligent people like yourself. They are among friends so they can be frank about their work, their joys, their sorrows, their worries, their wants, their warts. And time after time in these far ranging interviews, one rediscovers the fact that for many people writing is one of the most rewarding jobs on earth. For example, after visiting Israel he envisions it as both a garrison state and a cultivated society, both Spartan and Athenian. Israel tries to do everything, to understand everything, to make provisions for everything. Maybe he means to flatter her, though there was some interest in her writing, to establish something, though he doesn't know exactly what, for the times he would have to visit that city. Because once in the saddle, the new middle class abolishes the holidays and replaces the week of seven days with that of ten, in order that the people may no longer have more than one rest day out of ten. It emancipates laborers from the yoke of the church to more effectively subjugate them under the yoke of work. Until he does finally meet her and watches the motions of her and that circle, the distrust, the cruelty masked as eccentricity or disinterest, the shabbiness of these lives or careers—as some would call them—nothing very different from the advances and declines in the lives of office managers and postal clerks. So to operate the bank, push lever on base near hunter's legs. Teddy Roosevelt will lower his head, take aim and fire the coin into the opening in the tree trunk. Up pops angry grizzly bear. All resources, all facilities are strained. Unremitting thought about world situation parallels defense effort. These people in Israel are actively, individually involved in universal history. Nothing less than the accommodation of a million hands clapping a million feet keeping time to the up-down in-and-out of arteries expanding with something like pure vision and regret. At the Congress of Charities held in Brussels, one of the wealthiest of French industrialists declares to the applause of his colleagues: 'We are introducing certain methods of diversions for the children. We teach them to sing during their work, also to add and subtract. This distracts them and makes them accept bravely those twelve hours of labor necessary to procure their means of existence.' Since here the purest art is performed in absolute silence, visualized before being seen a singer with no song a world without end. Amen. To reset the bank, push back gun sight, push bear's head down into tree trunk. Lower green leaves and place another coin flat on gun barrel.

A Note on the 'Events"

At this point the activity of writing poetry and, of course, the poem itself, are not self-defining.
    The verbal machine left by the modernists holds a tentative relationship to whatever it is we call language. The poem's linguistic situation—that area of human activity described by the poem's use of language—has become marginal, no longer including much of the self-justifying energy that we, like all dutiful post-modernists, have been more than willing to ascribe to it.
    In his satires, William Burroughs has described the problems posed by the atrocities of media and pop culture. But, while in Burrough's assemblages the most evident procedure is the disjunction of the material, the opposite is true of these 'Events'. The rupture of sensibility chronicled by Burroughs in the 50s and 60s has by now become a given. One's instinctive response is not to balk at the fragmentation of cultural activity immersing us—e.g. reading an art or movie review while in front of the television while skimming a biography while attempting to sustain talk with the person next to you on the sofa—but instead to repair this disassociation to make some connection among the fragments.
    In choosing to play with this phenomena, I find my poetry redefining itself in terms of language and, even more important, containing a criticism of itself and, in turn, a criticism of the language it is defined by.
    Then, like the Mayan serpent, poems begin to swallow their own tails. Sections or lines from poems discarded several years ago, even work-in-progress, become animated within the landscape of a particular 'Event'. So new topographies and contexts are generated, which poetic language may now situate or be situated by.

(November 1976)

Another You
[1978-1979]
1981

SCAPES

1

random as mountains of arid wind
above a clack
a high noon of
tin cans and chaparral
lowered Chevys and holler
hurry up
get back in the
clack clack across nowhere faster
than what had been bearably
random as

2

vitals say lung or brain tissue weighed for significant trace of substances say
lead or any foreign matter deposited say in the air asymptomatic in children say
chronic fatigue or occasional loss of memory general defects in say maybe even

3

profit
or the memory of wealth
which is to say capital
or the memory of the body of the lord
which makes it November
shivering dusty nights
and almost anybody's ball game

4

crossed out vase of week old flowers nowhere the terror of a word that begs
terror getting this far and no farther than the nonsense of windows growing
thicker and no farther than 'thicker' so vague and pervasive the windows brittle
as calluses as windows after all are terror after all the tickets have been sold

does it speak is it smile and play back your words often as you need to talk out
of both sides of the image you have of arriving home to a replay of your smile
out of both sides of the image you have of your [words]

6

a flight up at least 50 years of polished wood he remembers something more
than would he make it another place another time better suited to ambulances
or elephants or shoulders dancing upstairs to the top of that voice yelling "get
a job"

7

cockeyed hey don't make me laugh there are some men strapped right to a tree
look sport how bad can it be even if they say you don't use Englsih so good it's
only been 12 years what do you expect of her come on kid there's birds in the
air wind in the leaves what else do you need to die

8

she calls of what she calls
little but the dance of bright commerce
at the extraordinary edges of things

9

is this 'dance' this 'commerce' escape from that other commerce not so brilliant
in the eyes he heard her whisper look at his eyes though he looks and sees
nothing more precipitous than the room at his back the moon outside swollen
with hot wind he thinks what he thinks fragile is no more so than on my knee
her asking for the old lyrics those rhymes to God she asks what God is is he
Fifi

10

'moon outside' why come back to it is Fifi not enough swelling with the nonsense of a vision of a daughter's voice is not enough Fifi pregnant with never why these things these outside moon desert wind these

11

fragile seems enough what it says though who on earth can imagine what it says they're doing here must be yes or here must be the same words the same place keep coming up in a snarl contrived to simply get behind us cut away what they're doing here yes or no

12

or not saying yes or no about writing about the habit of everyday more glass getting so you can't screw or look out at a hillside without the definite feeling you've arrived here before the ambiguous use of repetition maybe the glass or a conversation in the next room seems unfortunately like the one interrupted last time he looked in the mirror to say yes or

13

to exclude certain words to stare into dog's eyes Jack eyes dark brown human name to stare excluding all that stares back because he doesn't stare but the skyline does the Ford station wagon rolling uphill yes or no

14

unless it's the wind we're trying but what humor is there in that midget planting his fingers on the big blonde's thigh with or without cigar the midget that is maybe the blonde it doesn't matter to the 12 women who telephone voracious protest of objects rendered from the hubris of gnomes the largesse of full-hipped short-waisted o what has become of the morality of rain who will raise a voice against the infamy of drainpipes yes or no

15

though even in purple the most prosaic drainpipe demands that we need and what we get even if it's a glimpse through a dog's minute we leave the words out to stare again at the roofs the skyline reflected palm trees brilliant clouds reflected the rocking chair and French windows on the TV screen growing dark in the west

16

if wrested is truly what words are certain of the 'mouthful of air' each takes a menu glances across the freeway at a glass of ice water where the voices the traffic sense the gaping mouth of what we might momentarily stop for a [breath] of

17

tentative little indians true or false the spines of the palm or is it an evergreen or do we navigate a sea of blood sharply do they bleed do we come to begin again always at the same time strolling uphill hand in hand shifting gears down to the memory of those shoes we smiled in the library 12 years ago on home this is no place to think of dying read the street signs it isn't raining yet

18

guilty as charged but how and to whom and for how long can she remember the pain here a name there a name everywhere my father pours he says don't go out in the rain they say it's snoring cats and dogs straight from Chinese mushroom clouds they claim it perfectly safe as far as they know in the past it's always been the same story forgive the pain but not the lies about the stains on the shirt the egg flower the sweet and sour the paper-wrapped rain

19

from the bus window far as the eye can frame bar after bar of wheat alfalfa oats occasional barn or horse resting dark against green choruses of the eye receding to the presently cruel conclusions of this [   ]

sketch might be the word left out as the bumps the peaches the olive rows that
are not green but bearably symmetric this time of year 12 years ago

21

[t]eurat. tanna. la. rezus ame vachr lautn. aatiuth: arvasaapha. al. aalchuvaiseraturannuve. velthinas. e stla. afunas sleleth caru tezan. fusleri. ri. athi. litiltalipilekatur. anuvecimima _ _ _ matesi. lesns teis rasnes. ipa ama hen naper XII. araturanuve. velusi. velthinaturas. cras. pe ras cemulm lescul zuci. en esci. epl tularu. siikanzich.

and left with talking and space and
an uncertain intensity
between maybe and someone and
deep flies in the blaze and gusty
February of outfielding
and outfields want time and space and syntax and a
propinquity for being specific about what nobody's
hands on the
foot on the
say hey can you see
who's on first and

.

she turns and says to him remember it well she is what her friends called her she says 'next time we won't talk so much will we' until he wants to take her [pale] neck between his fingers and not because he was told to button it but that she used that terrifyingly first plural as their friends called it in those days assuming he was looking at her curly head pink hands too large eyes and writhing cigarette and assuming he was even there to talk today remember it well today is what their friends used to

.

hey can you says is seeing all you cannot empirically but in fact in the eye yes in the eye all you can hope to touch husband to land earth to sky high as the eye yes the eye can says you do and some says you do what you don't really says you see the aye is a feel you have for seeing what you says we're not I says we're not talking about what you says really but seeing what you says you love when you sees it until it dances up to you like the sun the size of a barn and you can't get it out of your eyes no matter how bad you closes them or shakes your head for wishing you had said it first

∙

regardless of whether you is 34 or left handed or a preordained factor in an already known movement or tendency away from whether you is neither here nor there because you is what you's expected to say yes or some to say no but always under the sun almighty yes because it's only opinions that count among the no-account and the best who are blessed in the land of was should and forever will be yes and more yes from bumper to shining bumper yes let us hear it from the brother in the back there with his head tucked under his arm yes let him ride through our night swinging those lantern righteous eyes because yes he is one of us sifting the likely from the unlikely and yes though we says no and no though we says yes it's always yes for the brother it's always yes for the sister it's always yes for the lover riding his headless ride through the selfhood of this dark and yes this dark and yes this dark and

∙

and when we walk
and when we stand
and when we smile
and when we sit
and when we talk
and when we tell
and when we sing
and when we reach
and when we stop
and when we go
and when we stumble
and when we look
and when we bend
and when we touch
and when we pause
and when we blink
and when we itch
and when we scratch
and when we hurry
and when we don't
and when we wait
and when we whistle
and when we stretch
and when we listen
and when we turn
and when we start
and when we should
and when we break
and when we run
and when we chase
and when we leap

•

and the mystery in fat is on the bone and the meanwhile in fact a bastard to live since a question of a woman he danced until eight years before he could dance with in short a habit of say a small house and a play on her words he thought was dead however grave he hears his own doubts turning over in the meantime of his sleep of a steep wind and deep grass and her sea gray eyes of westerly matter-of-fact afternoons they always together with the third the small because in a very consequently thicket of silence as it burns as always tangerine while they together he dreams although of his own mouth

•

too steep to abandon to sight beyond the wheel of a purple loading and reloading thumb and forefinger sighted over the windshield of a grimy sleeping bang bang pair of precisely within a pinch of here comes everybody looking like hell was yesterday and there's no time left on the meter to brush teeth walk dog scratch ass to look in the mirror for the crack in the glass in the dream sighted along a very thin line of regret

•

and she says and he picks up the glass and she says and he closes his eyes and she says and he stirs the soup and she says and he looks at the spoon and she says and he leans back from the table and she says and he gets to his feet and she says and he looks around for the salt and pepper and she says and he moves back to the table and sits down and she says and he drops some salt in his hand into the soup and she says and he shakes some pepper into the bowl and she says self-respect and he picks up the spoon and she says self-respect and he puts down the spoon and she says and he gets to his feet takes two steps to the refrigerator and she says and he opens the refrigerator and reaches for a beer and she says and he takes two steps back to the table removes a glass from the cupboard sits down and she says and he pours the beer and she says and he watches the head rise in the glass and she says and he stands quickly eight steps to the door twists the double-lock eight steps back and she says and he sits down and she says and he looks at his glass of beer and she says and he looks at his soup and she says and he picks up his spoon and begins

•

or whatever possesses him to purple such waking of mirrors peeking through medicine cabinets within an inch of making absolutely no matter how many times he repeats the departure like hell was yesterday and there's no meter left to time the brushing of teeth the walk of a dog the scratch of an ass the length of a very thin

•

and begins to change pronouns midstream out the feet and ears as if nodding off to pay the piper were not the piper but a spoon of a different color it however you wait it can't mean it isn't enough to awake indefinitely and suppose as far as you can throw it consisting it was all a long way to his own mouth

•

boxcars belch the foggy tick
chopping each off the figures of
anyway he likes it
metaphor vision
don't mean a thing
if it ain't what he means
not what he means
but what he means when he wakes
and no one's there to listen

•

through the light rain in Glendale he wakes
in Wrocław has to be Wrocław
when it's always been Glendale
far as Glendale means what he means
in Glendale
if he means no one there at all to

•

the test of the story seeing
that sure of Wrocław
gray like damp like
railroad sounds like
at least a [thought, heart,
etc.] he saw Glendale waking
close as his [   ] on the floor
the torn [   ] in the corner
the ring of the disconnected
[   ] under the bed

.

ridding the ate of hearts or the inedible rereading of a goodly spoon renegoti-
ating the thought of a start a beginning an ending up synonymous in a differ-
ent week than the one run through the fingers of downtown [   ] yes or

.

the rest of the story reading
footsteps cough through the wall
fingers buttocks
words scratched out
the salty roomful of sweet pain
and parentheses
jerked wide open
the eyes swallowed
of the final syllable whistles between delicious teeth

AN ELEGANCE FOR DODA

Carol Doda, queen of silicone and topless dance; an imprint of her notorious glands was donated to the city of San Francisco.

even the sidewalk
discovers your breast
and if you were old
you are young
and if you were lost
you are found
buried tomorrow
in your snapshot of bones
own token of flesh
to the tips of your toes
the mountain crows
the sun shakes
even a tree knows
the moon speaks but once
and like sand flows
through the eyes of the dead
the clamor of snow
even a tree knows
the moon speaks but once
and like sand it snows
in the eyes of the dead
in the breast of the young

ANOTHER YOU

> "Find a new world; a new world is necessary. But I meant a new word."
> – Madame O

and which about some of it deserves
e.g. prosody like

turn for this reason
one found finds requires roses to read

who maybe even
who knows or
who when not only when but who

though even the most one finds indefinitely
paying the vague price
sometimes e.g.

but there is however space
two lines to be shortly possible
that [I] [he] approaches

    •

a willing suspension of apples
bobbing like friars in the grass
what's the score
why always steel blue eyes to love
does it hurt anymore to slice
little women from the disbelief
of yet another pose of roses

    *

a medium
a sentimentality
of beginning out of time
out of place
forgetting how to seem
in the wide open spaces of
[nostalgia] [willfulness] [surprise]
pick one
you'll never be another you

*

in the face of memory
as if something was to spit out
how unskillfully or fully enough
the record followed to the last dot
she says jubilant that she says
that he says that I say that
after all language is after all
is said and all the camels have
squeaked through the eye of your rose

*

here I sit brokenhearted
fruitless on a throne of air
to jar your cloudiness
or my banality
your partridge in a pear
my plum in the waiting for you
or is it o you beautiful doll
you great big beautiful
or is it

*

turn for any reason not pages
but the sentiment of paper
remember it like a rose
inches from the hopelessly perfect
of one voice you'll wake
and forget to just
picking sighs of the pillowcase
because yes we've got no bananas
we've got none because today

Gof in Singapore
[1982]
1983

and a voice is more often a voice of outside the voice is as she screams turning
left in front of a hot May Friday 4:30 in the 'Wait for me' as she screams
hunger without appetite silence with no margin for the thirsty faces the
crowding as she screams Wafer me away from the page that was sacrificed this
afternoon

•

he misses the bus more often than not he remembers what he forgot to say and
is left with having to forget the living to remember to scream stop the bus and
let my brother Jack more often than not the page is ripped out as the hands are
read and remembered in the dark rocking trolley as all the lights go off and
outside the voices it's bright midnight tentative little indians ago who never
screams get a job

•

did he miss the bus or not says she
felicitous as a snake in rayon
the phone rings he loses his place
she dials a number no one answers
the bus is packed he has to fart
she changes the subject he doesn't dare
the phone rings a page is missing
can't reach the chord it blows away
misses his stop she changes the subject
doesn't dare the bus is packed
the phone rings a page is missing

•

it blew away but not that simple
a necktie maybe or an old friendship
depending on the choice of sunsets
what's left to hold the sox up
a nostalgia or even a rage for justice
as the metaphors now seem nothing more
loud bands lots of heroes cheap gas
a piece of cake as they demonstrate in Singapore

•

is it to keep alive
that luminous torso that radiant step
when the slope above the freeway is alive
pubic with mesquite and chaparral
do we remember the words
do we keep our dead understood
and dancing parenthetically
as sparrows dance those ripe tunes
in foggy hibiscus

•

is it strictly for the record for the living who make a living playing the record backwards who incriminate the whispers they couldn't fear in case the singer is without a song as she cuts in front of this mute Friday voiceless behind her windshield mouthing words she never thought to mouth Wafer me as she plays her car backwards into the parking lot rolls up her window screaming what she couldn't hear

•

literally it was a week ago

what she couldn't hear was the quiet of this table

what she didn't know would destroy her

how she was dressed doesn't matter

that it was Friday afternoon and her about 30 was convenient

that it's a glass table is worth mentioning

that it gleams with accusation is redundant

why the bare leg and slipper under the table look so disembodied isn't really important

that she blocked traffic to push a button to slide her window down to scream what she screamed is only coincidental

it was literally one week ago he had to fart and a page was missing

•

windows still dirty birdsong acute
everything else shrinks in the ripening wind
lavender pickup garbage cans mailman
telephone ringing in the next room
and the luminous torso the radiant step
naming the motion of the oak
as it removes all movement but memory

*

as if one poises to plunge that perfect whiteness
when the page is in fact not white
and anybody's business but the living
because the birds won't shut up the knee hurts so
he's furious at even the thought of yesterday or her
changing the subject as he considers chasing the bus

*

the ache revises the birdsong more acute
the writing fast and sloppier
dove swoop the size of a pigeon
the street outside is nobody's business
indian brush and oak and tile roofs
stir terribly slow as a Sunday afternoon
when all vision subsides to ash
and mother rises to answer the telephone

*

he moves to the kitchen easy as breath
she hands him parenthetically a cup of coffee
they talk of gophers or cacti or Wittgenstein
she asks if he wants to hear her dream
anybody in the rest of the house is sound asleep
they talk of gilia or desert or Husserl
he says he'd like to go fishing soon
she carefully describes letters she avoids writing
the phone rings a page is ripped out
it's years before they talk of dreams again

*

Connemara Delphi Kinshasa Corlaga Fundy Manhattan Fort-Lamy or Perth

they often appear to be looking straight ahead the cord missing

or every few weeks the small anonymous envelope of rubber bands from Van Nuys

not mornings of eager light brief passages and gliding etc.

or canceled checks from Singapore always made out to cash always those ink stains under the signature

•

they circle not seeming to move the feet
only eyes and lips splendid with hunger
the phone rings as the throat is cut
the page ripped out as blood covers the hands
and the voices approach call out names
he tries to remember the words
the radiant step the phone rings
as they circle thirst like flame
does he dare to sing

•

Bath Bangkok Bamabo Baikal. The phone stops. His hands are red. Even birthday greetings from Patagonia, six months late, unsigned: a worn looking penguin squints on the front of the card, some script inside praising 'Gof and Gof's children.' The phone rings again. The eyes are wide open. And of course the canceled checks, regular as the familiar almost paw-like stain under the signature. The phone stops. The room and furniture seem larger. Sobat Satahip Sugari Singapore Solo Shan.

•

the room photographs somewhat empty the furniture a
little word and oversize

everything quite neat though as if arranged once more
at the last minute

some faces look almost smug fingers around half-empty
glasses but no legs crossed

their hands all the same none match the heads and seem
larger than they should

that the table gleams slightly isn't remarkable

the phone they said rang twice then stopped

one definitely needs a shave quite a few have their
shoes off

it's been more than a week now the time of day probably
makes no difference

most of all the eyes seem relieved tranquil marmorial or
just startled by the propriety of the instant

·

a household of names and dates unfurnished except for a few platitudes and a
funeral someone keeps mentioning nobody's in the kitchen shaving and only
his daughter runs through the garden anyhow time accumulates rumor persists
even if most endings remain minor and the reader to blame again for being
reread

·

It was crowded and too dark. The clock above the door read six sharp but it had to be a lot later. The hatcheck girl made funny little smiles at my tall package and me but I ignored her. Most of them were there, at tables in the corners, trying not to be conspicuous. They looked the other way and the smart people they sat with kept on chattering. Sometimes you get a hunch what the talk is about but this place was different. I worked the package and myself casually as I could toward a couple of empty seats and Whitman at the end of the bar. Nice thing about Walt, he was always where you expected. For instance, trying to maneuver some amateur into a devastating contradiction or at least a compliment or two and a free beer. Anyhow, muscular freshman from Princeton weren't what I'd come for so I slapped old Walt on the back, got him to laugh that laugh of his and took a stool on his other side. Mostly got a lot of Walt's shoulder which was just fine with me. As I said the next stool was empty but on the bar in front of it almost a full glass sat like some kind of shrine. Strawberries, champagne, etc. In Paris they called it a Nymphe, in Rome a Paradiso. Don't know why but I got so curious I almost reached over and touched it. When its owner walked up I flinched as if I had. It wasn't so much the surprise but the fact she took my breath away. Five-ten in loafers, long blond hair, no makeup, straight nose, high forehead and those gray eyes. They had more than a touch of smoulder to keep you mesmerized and exquisite enough for no one else to notice. Pure class. Didn't even inquire about the package, just if I might not want to prop it in the corner next to her, which I did. Her talk was effortless or maybe it was the way she got me going. She asked questions and more than once I was amazed at my answers. She must have ordered another one of those drinks because I found the thing in my hand toasting who knows what. No matter how hard I try, it's only been a week, I can't remember at all what we said. It was more like a dance than anything else. She led and I followed and I didn't give a damn. Anyhow, at that point, right after the toasts, something happened. I glanced over toward Whitman and was a little surprised. Instead of grinning and well on his way, Walt was quiet, elbows on the bar, kind of examining his beer. The kid looked at Walt as if he'd said something and was expecting an answer. Somehow that made me nervous. I started to look around at the tables. They were gone. Strangers had taken their places, sat at their chairs. I needed to talk and they disappeared. As I turned back to her, I swear I felt something coming. She looked at me with a question on that perfect face of hers. If she spoke I didn't hear. I was in no mood for conversation. The bar rail under my feet was pitching and rolling and I knew I'd never learn the steps. I started to reach for my package. She was smiling and had her arms around me, breaking my fall, when the lights went out.

a small breeze again this morning
though the sparrows are already quiet
traffic hums a sign along the dry hills
it's mid-July postcard flesh on roller skates
the Pacific about 17 miles to the southwest
he stares at the doorway
tomorrow he dreams of never having known you before

Rime
[1983]
1984

RIME (rime) n. hoarfrost, frozen mist, chill mist or fog; accumulation of granular ice tufts on the windward side of exposed objects formed by super-cooled fog or cloud and built out directly against the wind; crust, encrustation. — tr.v. *rimed, riming, rimes.* To cover with or as if with rime; to pry; to count, number, reckon, recount; (obs.) to make clear, to clear away. (ME *rim*, OE *hrim*.) — *rimy* adj.
RIME Variant of *rhyme*.

scalding what the doctor called a 'minor sprain'
brandy and soda on a chair telephone
unplugged towel folded on toilet lid
inscribe those afternoons that inflamed October
even the turf in Kezar Stadium
once a week undefeated we lost our voices
for a team that never seemed to lose
most names and faces maybe purposefully
forgotten a few like Mike or Al
livid as corned beef thumping Jerry
on the back who always looked about to swoon
those perfect seasons now two decades past
a different heat steams my glasses
a different season fires my bath

morbid tint of glass the hooker's glance
the crossed-out phrases the mechanical ass
oasis of Arabs hawking t-shirts and maps
a hag at the bus stop eighty-nine degrees
blonde curls castled in an eternity of
shopping bags three teenage girls wiggling
and waving from the back of a pickup
Vietnamese peddling luggage in a parking lot
peroxide boys demonstrating shaved armpits
and swell teeth a smart redhead in sunglasses
cop with cigar a dead cat at the sewer
who wouldn't play the occasional king
desert lover demon wind to jolt mountains
decree the air this sharp steel blue

unless the unearthly be unforgiven
the unquestionable unanimous
unstable unabridged unsatisfied
ash of the acceleration of rhyme
when is the unquenchable table
the spill of a hand twice upon mine
how my hand this undulating impudence
this impotence indifference to time
and I why do I wait for the scream
send each morning fresh stains to be forgiven
el pueblo de la reina de los ángeles
maybe if the itch of a fervent window
the want of a hard G never a soft

who can deny a city that gives nothing back
where the rain always leaves at night
and only leprechauns and gaffers
whistle at the end of a rainbow
who can deny the sincerity of
hot dog stands envisioned as hot dogs
checks emblazoned with skiers and
snow-capped Sierras who can deny
a communion of lovers at eighty
miles per hour shot once through the head
a replay of roses of ten million
sincere words still missing still arriving
to die among strangers once and for all

dry and redundant
as cold November
sky are skin
light and french
window are
feathers I deny
your fervent neck
this beak that
won't give or
spend the heat
of the little there
is to write of
skin light and
french window

in the scalding tub dipping black hairs
from the water remembering the *Commedia*
those stories of British Columbia
1905 the cousin who ventured
40 below mid-blizzard to crap
while the others huddled in the tent
Pasquale my grandfather intoning
Dinanzi a me NON FUOR COSE CREATE
SE NON ETTERNE, E IO ETTERNA DURO.
LASCIATE OGNI SPERANZA, VOI CH'ENTRATE
and cousin never returned until the next day
when the blow let up about thirty paces
from the tent spotted his boots dark as sin
in the new snow the feet still in them

7

I sang and sang and nothing else would do
asleep in my wallet a radio belches
a sad song or two and nothing else
I lisp awake the oleander satisfied
I delete the blanket wet my lips
I nibble small hair and suck the din
of what she doesn't say I forget
her name I forgive no one but myself
as many times as necessary
to forget how often I've listened
even for a breath hers mine those burning
songless nights I was afraid she'd stepped
across brushed off that immensity and
left me shamed and gawking in my sleep

fickle cypresses Juno is in heat
as arid now a season as any
more or less comfortable with clouds
and nobody's to redeem the dead kittens
vomit demons on your rocking chair
someday of course German may again
become the esperanto of the streets
you read me Jack the boys are off to college
mother's on retreat it's just us and them and
cartoons on the windshield of a '62 Dodge
to steer the tongue westerly decode ashes
of remorse arouse the insurrection
of innocence after all who ever said
we could take the heat of inspiration

9

flagrant periscope Pluto in retreat
as tepid a wind as the whimsy
of a feather that unframes the story crowds
attention if only because what's written
doesn't snare what's seen so to speak is air
heavier than matter or any terrain
of rhyme even the agile sweetmeats
the fragrant passages of pleasure knowledge
stands isolate hence useless to memorize
a list of survivors to lodge
protest with the sublime when its lashes
envisioned on the lens of time nations
of whispers lies that demand not to be read
silences that are no less incrimination

10

are the cumulus so heavy the stew
doesn't boil Persephone just belches
the shrews won't rut I incite a face
with windows and dictionary satisfied
to outscribble buses read the lisp
of a pen indite what could have been
on the back of an envelope beset
a memory or two catch myself
rewriting 'clearly' less like 'dearly'
wipe sweat off the scalp as it glistens
December late afternoon a yearning
sudden and liquid as if I'd paused to step
off the boulevard into an alley and
begun to talk to you in my sleep

as this syllabus of remorse dares
the season as this late Arcadia
forges memory tries even the umbra
of desire each day unlike the heart captures
more light grows warmer pajama and shirt flap
on the clothesline any previous intent
purely temperamental not bemoaning
as some would have it all that artifice
Buscas en Roma a Roma, ¡oh peregrino!
y en roma misma a Roma no la hallas
what splendor remains antipasto for
senator or semiologist in that face
of a busboy big dusky eyes that slight grin
wavers a shadow of this mausoleum

nothing incumbent after the rain
least not the caliber
of dreams a skin
of adjectives the hunch
of barking sleep are
tabled this dry
morning this lingering wreck
of a passage that
vanishes at the door
rings like fresh meat
spills the busy air
swells the coloratura of
the refrigerator and
dwells in the cruelty of a rainbow

Hippolyta at the door I lack
nerve and gulp a window or two of light
laving the flaxen small hair at the nape
of her neck or nucha my crisp window
within a translation of a translation of
too brief a time too much memory logged
at this glass table if to sing in one's head
is to lavish rhyme an extravagant lie
of not wanting to forget then these ready
syllables are better forgotten than read
or best bled of all rememberings one by one
letting their fluent mooring divesting
this want of even the timbre of a giggle

l'odorino amaro nel cuore driven
not so much to taste but to restore
the sheer profusion the bittersweet ride
awash in an instant of light if time
instead translates the heart one's unable
you say to prevent history undermine
a countenance of whispers or the sublimely
misplaced continent of a past and since
these rhymes may soon disappoint seeming
little more than the quiver of a drunken
hand judge what cruel hope the rain obliges
and your own eyes carissima that tango
the headlong discipline of diguise

15

today at last big with spring I glance
across the street your missing rosy
lips along my fingers leaves and stems
of this spider plant a livid filigree
of morning the time and again of
rising from that table the door framing
bushy low hills traffic hum the abrupt
and final sense of a boy's ocean forgot
and speechless the oak doesn't stir bits
of green fall from my hand you're here I glance
again my glasses dusty I lower
my eyes turn from the doorway king
of this moment already past fountains
of light at my feet the wall a slight blue

Villa
[1983-1986]
1991

"My mind is utterly unlike my body, and, unless you are a god, so I am certain is yours."

-- Hadrian

Preface

Who, if not a secretary, is more apt to savor a neatly turned epistle? Who, if not a chronicler, might more easily be excused making public what was meant as private? And still the more so, if he has never shunned the intimate event in treating of the general. What was personal and nugatory may gain resonance in the public forum. The tesserae of the smallest pavement may find just place in the grandest villa.

Shunning Clodian fashion, our correspondent signed himself in the antique manner: PAULLUS, born under a waning moon. Yet his virtue seems more of our time than of our ancestors'. My dismissal and distance from the imperial court first made me safeguard his Tiburtine missives. Of late I have discovered that, happily, others had done the same. The assembled memoranda may now open windows, however narrow, where otherwise would be a wall. A chronicle they are not, though here they follow chronologically.

Or at least they follow in such an order as could be recalled by their recipients. There occurs an unaccountable lapse, it should be noted, of almost a year between VIII and IX. The last four, XXX-XXXIII, must have been written, the one upon the other, in the days immediately after the Emperor's death. Two further notes: notwithstanding its recipient's claim to the contrary, one cannot help but consider letter II fragmentary-- a second page, or a conclusion to a longer communication. I have honored Marcellus' dating of the circumstantial letter XVII, although the references to the 'Feast of Fools' (which one would take to be the Lupercalia) and my own *Of Notable Whores* cast it into some doubt. At best, one must assume that the host of that festival deemed necessary to fete the Fool more than once a year-- so doing in late July!
Valete!

– G. Suetonius Tranquillus

I

Dearest Fabritius, it has been
almost five month you've been gone.
Already your name leaves gaps
even in smart conversation.
A few more months and you will be
like the classics graciously
forgotten. I stand at the door
awkward with what to say to you.
My eyes are on a sparrow
exploring the garden and I
confess my mind serves no better
than to compare your self-exile
to the sparrow's hop. You claim
life goes on, you and I the kind
who always pull through and the rest
of your platitudes. That you are
probably right it all turns to
chatter and we come back for more
is what disappoints even
at times disgusts me. In this room
six months from now, watching the upraised
heads of the nymphaea chasing
October clouds, the two of us
gallantly drunk over this period
of our lives, like some Cauchian sea
we braved as young men. We pause
as if to sniff the air, the nymphs
elegant and alert, a slight
breeze. The prospect saddens me
indescribably. I'm up again
pacing the room. The sparrow's gone.
It's not quite ten o'clock. The gardens
are still fresh, certainly fresher
than my thoughts. I will take a walk.
Your best friend, etc.

II

Again, my winter rose, that shame
of being unable to love enough
in return, when a moment later
you blush, your fear mounts, you urge
I must kiss you at least a thousand
times before saying goodnight
and sleep steals you from me. So why
allude to the Emperor or
my age? Like the dark that yawns
in our faces, time and the Caesars
will be favored. We serve with each breath,
with every thrust of wit we play
their song. So why be reminded
of necessity? I stop here.
The hour nibbles. Caesar prepares
for his morning bath and reading.
In any case, please come. Perhaps
tonight, or slip into my chamber
tomorrow with the first light.
We will exchange kisses buoyant
as your years and linger and laugh
like sister and brother like the prince
and princess we were meant to be.
I remain ever what you will,

III

Dear Master Enculpius, regarding
the disposition of the Asian pool,
I am sure you appreciate these are not
simple questions of architecture or taste
but the very fabric of empire. Caesar
needs, unlike us, to enshrine, to mirror
the abundance of his imagination,
else he would be fixed in the mundane
and niggling cares that press unfortunately
on our lesser brows. Your insistence
on what you call 'classic values' is,
if I may say so, peripheral. The great task
is the Emperor's. Like the education
of a mind, space is ultimately his
to shape. The monument in question
may be only the syllable of a dream,
this window the product, perhaps, of a sigh.
In short, Caesar needs counsel and friendship,
not instruction. Excuse my frankness
but surely you are more than aware that
our vision is not isolate but, like the
scintilla of a fountain, dependent
on his effulgence for whatever splendor
we may gather in this life. Please, try him
sparingly. Use the patience which, no doubt,
you have cultivated in the long practice
of your art. I must tell you I assume
such frankness more than anything as an
admirer, an occasional student of
the mastery you lend to the coincidence
of water and stone. In closing I trust
you will append to this rude admiration
the understanding that my remarks go
no further than this page. Respectfully,
I await your reply,

IV

My Fortunatus,
how are the idylls
of Neapolis?
Does the frigate bird still
overtake his shadow,
is the starfish so
unyielding, the arch
of her foot so generous
to keep you from my letters?
Here I must pause before your
happiness. I bear a question,
more like the pebble one rubs
in one's pocket as a boy.
To antipose the Greek:
poet, what of the light?
If we must, as you insist,
avert suffering, if to pain
is useless, if in struggle
we don't transcend but repeat
as in a waking dream
blown deeper and deeper
into a tunnel
of self-absorption,
what do we learn? Surely
not just to sit and wait.
If the best or worst,
as you say, requires
no belief, why learn at all?
Or is one never too old
to overreach, to hope
for dispensation
from his daily bread,
embracing in the cool of
first light her broad shoulders,
her drowsy back. Then
the pale dawn, false dawn
as fisherman call it,

involves us in the most
relentless dream of all.
This, my friend, the pity.
To wish to maintain that light
if only in the merest
fountain of syllables,
to want to husband
and grow old with it,
as if age were simply
a journey from A to B.
I break off here, excessive
in my stay and frame of mind.
I leave you to those
devotions that in sublime
fervor and single-mindedness
outshine the most fanatic
Christian or Jew. I hope,
though not from envy
on my part, to hear from you
soon. I remain your own
all to stubborn creature
of his sensibilities,

V

Of course, Marcellus, sleep doesn't 'steal'
her from me. If anything, it is more
like pilfering. But sentiment, my dear,
even, I suspect, our deepest feelings
often thrive on the verge of banality.
You do not suppose we were the first
to discover the dawn infiltrating
our chamber, the small light playing on the nose
of the beloved. In any case, the self
has always seemed to me a misplaced notion.
The deeper one goes the more mundane,
the less uncommon one's perceptions.
Plato has written: the eyes of a lover
are like a million stars. No sentiment
but fact. Compared to her infinity
of glances, that precocious blue of her eyes,
the Milky Way is only a toy.
I am afraid we must look elsewhere
than the self. The heart, my friend, gathers
no wisdom only pain and ecstasy.
One learns to treat it like a pocket,
sometimes full, others almost empty
but always, one hopes, there is something
for it to bear. I thank you for your comments.
If not repairing my style, they are at least
a diversion in an otherwise stagnant
morning. As ever, a warm embrace,

VI

My mouth, my eyes, as the Africans
plead, why do your words confuse me?
You've been away barely a month
and our letters seem to dangle
over a chasm. Dearest, why must you
immerse your life in parables,
keeping so much, as you call it,
'elemental,' beyond questioning?
Tell me, is the answer that obviuos?
My vain and naive heart, I regret,
grows redundant as the heat.
My body sleeps little, eats less,
drinks almost no wine and wishes
no other body than your own.
These last words I've crossed out three times.
They stay more than anything out of
some perverse notion of our friendship.
In the bloated heat, the veins
of this table cool and merciless,
my fingers estranged in considering
how to translate the dead quiet
that swells and inflames.
It crowds me. I must close. I am,
as ever, stubbornly yours,

VII

If to father is to bequeath the light,
I leave only lies to wriggle in the sun
Like worms inch across the flagrant ledge
Of who I will never be.

My dear Gaius, I advance a scrap
of some unfinished verse as
affidavit of my displeasure and
frustration with you. In your letters
you are preoccupied always
with challenging my age, recalling
your precocity and my
complacency or complicity
with the moon and stars, how I'm content,
as you say, to 'play by chance';
how dire, instead, your genius
as it imbibes the very ooze of
Hades, etc. etc.
But with me why must you play
the desperate Spaniard? Why approach
your talent like some grand footrace
among the slaves of the first families
of Rome? The race, my Gaius,
has no beginning, middle or end.
We carry home no prizes except
our defeat, and the rules strike as
arbitrary as a young woman's
caresses. What you take for my
absence of determination
is an impatience with myself;
the lack of grace to turn a phrase
as I know it might be turned,
a reluctance to sit and write
so tormented by beauty and
her sulking mouth. But I will not
punish myself or, for that matter,
anyone else. I keep a distance.

Outside in the first light, nightwind
hurries the faces of the water.
The marble shoulders will come and sing
to me or they will not. If this
is chance I play at, so be it.
It is, like yourself, not an unworthy
opponent. As always,

VIII

How did the dog days treat you,
my dear Fortunatus?
Your only letter,
even that bit of verse on
the stoical inclination
of your Venus' chin,
was fanatically brief.
I must tell you it's not
just envy spurs my wit
but a mood of inventory,
a willful, almost devout
detachment, leaving
my days transparent,
if uneventful.
We've begun another study
of the Canopian pool,
what he now calls our 'Great Pool.'
Ill as he has become,
his body a quarreling
senate of pain, he grows
resolute as his fatal
adversary. Probably
I exaggerate this last phrase.
In fact, the few occasions
he's mentioned the little time
that remains, he simply spoke
of a conclusion or
coda, something of an
executor of his days.
But, Fortunatus,
I who am just the sum
of my aspirations?
What is to be my end?
Am I fingers only
and curls and splendid neck,
or drowsy afternoons
of promises and lost knives?

And when there are no more dreams
and promises, only the dreams
and promises of others?
The face of the Emperor
is on coins, buildings,
monuments, public baths.
Bravely he has preformed
his life, let the throne play
through him. I shun my face.
I pain to remove it,
to puke that smirking
orphans self into one of
these thousand pools and fountains.
Instead, drunk with speech,
I chatter and chatter,
adorn and elaborate
the mask. I write verses.
I lack the courage
to stop talking. We all die
like dogs you've often said.
Daily I watch the Emperor
die. Sometimes I attend him
when he rises, his eyes
urgent, his shoulders tensed
for the onslaught of pain,
the hands ready to grasp
the briefest moment of
unselfish thought. One late night,
most of us nodding in our
wine, he spoke half-jokingly of
his illness. If it grew worse
he would be forced, he said,
to post a guard near his bed,
to protect, as he put it,
the protector of the empire
from himself. Who, my dear friend,
will there be to protect us?
I remain, as always,

IX

My dear Fabritius,
a late and most famished
apology for a tacit
month. Fractions of light,
a whirl of flying ants,
pine needles' tick
on the marble table.
As I write I am keenly
almost hysterically
aware of these tired emblems.
Doubt and bitterness
overflow. A nostalgia
for quiet some way
fulfills this trinity.
Why, even to you,
must I seem a cloud in flesh
too vulgar, or a mind
quite easily ashamed
of its own reflection.
I stare toward the sea.
This morning the horizon
cannot conceal my dread
as it so often has.
I can't help seeing you
again in this chair
almost a year ago,
full of wine and metaphor,
shouting that God is Life.
The words are flaccid.
I seem unable to urge
my mind from the whisper
of this table. If to form
a question, even to wonder
becomes itself redundant,
why am I compelled so?
If your god is life,
is he or she not a

squalid and cruel god?
You talk of patience and
survival but, like me,
breakfast on last week's
misery, trusting our
pencils to go unnoticed
in the soft feast. If I were
to suspect or loathe you,
want secretly to be
rid of your friendship,
as I did my wife
and even perhaps now
my sweetest and hopeless love,
it's because none of you
can spare me, none can keep
the chill from my heart.

I have moved from my terrace to the schoolroom.
It is my weekly obligation to play
teacher, to educate the heirs of empire.
I sit before them scribbling in whitest
muslin and slippers, very much the part.
While my disdain grows, my reputation
for virtue and knowledge swells in extremis.
I gaze at the young faces bent over
the grammar I assigned to occupy
the two hours and allow me to finish this
and several other letters. Occasionally,
when a face looks up to take a breath,
to rest the writing hand, our eyes meet
and there's the impression he knows my secret,
why I'm here, staring blank faced at him
and his schoolmates. I begin to find a
kind of ease, even some inspiration
in their faces, though who can say how anxious
one is to be inspired. Truly, I must close.
The clepsydra tells me my lesson
is about to end. I require no answer,
only more of your excruciating patience.
As ever and ever,

X

My dear son, I must apologize for yesterday
being unable to meet you. Caesar at the last moment
needed counsel. The only messenger to be found
was new to Rome and, rather than admit so, he stumbled
two or three hours around the Capitoline before
coming back without having begged your pardon. I am disturbed
at what you must have thought of me and even more at not
seeing you and hearing of your adventures in the guards.
I think I have at last accepted the notion of you
as a soldier. This change of heart— one of the things I had wished
most to speak of yesterday— has colored the last few weeks
with some tranquility. News of your successes trickle down
to me through the cistern of official gossip and
I am eager for more. By now you may be wondering
why this interest in your career? Because of my youth
when you were born, or perhaps in an urge to prolong that youth,
I have always treated you more like a younger brother
than a son. But, in these last few months, I feel the advent
of something prodigious: to have you in your manhood
born to me again; to clarify, not confound my life,
as a stone hurled at bright noon across a canyon clarifies
tree and sky and rock. For a change, I sense time working
not entirely to my disadvantage. Yes, of course, I still
pamper my vices. As you can see when momentarily
not talking of myself, I must wax poetical. Amen.
As for public duties, soon I will be alone at court,
that is, without the drama of his imperial presence.
Caesar will travel, ill as he is, to erect one more
temple to the memory of his eternal love.
I remain to supervise construction. (In practice
my authority serves little more than obstructing
the arrogance of architects until Caesar returns.)
So much for the world as spectacle. My inner circus
is at a risky though not hopeless point. I would not say
things are exactly 'well' with Leucothea, though perhaps better.
(Better than what, I do not know. When I try to think of her,
it is as if I were strolling through a city of dreams

where faces are sweet and formal and some greet me by name
though they are complete strangers.) In any case, by fate
or divine intercession, our lives for the moment
intersect. She works harder and, it seems, more successfully
than ever on her study of music and dance. I am
in a different frenzy: inhabited of light,
marble pool, cypress, nympharum, stark dawn, frozen shoulders,
cloud and sun beyond adjective, chill swift day, night without end,
the green edge of sea vague and forgiving on the horizon.
And ever the stare, ever the scribble of the mind inching
not toward what I am or imagine but what I will never be.
In closing I spare you much fatherly advice. Be kind
and brave and, in these most ignoble of times, careful.
Incidentally, when you next visit the lady who is
your mother and was once my wife, please kiss her hands for me.
As always I embrace you and remain your father,

XI

Dearest, writing to you
I feel your gaze over
my shoulder, pointed
as the light about to reach
this table. You say
you will accept only
letters of love from me.
You say as we grow old
we necessarily change—
you and I, for example,
have changed much in these
two years. But to gain wisdom
because we have seen more,
simply because we age,
seems to me a hideous joke—
as unworthy of belief
as of a love letter.
If I might, instead,
turn your gaze from me,
pull you through the glass
of your smiles, glances, your
easy voice, you would see
why I am so driven,
as you often put it,
to annoy myself.
Here, then, a catalog
of your faults, both an open
window and a mirror,
yourself at the center,
in my biased glare.
Thus:
        impatient
        imperious
        impetuous
        imposing
extremely
        self-conscious,

lacking
    in confidence—
certainly not nerve,
    immaculate
    immovable
    impudent
    intolerant
glutton
    for affection,
harsh
    to the dearest,
sweetheart
    to acquaintances,
    impious
    impenetrable
    impressionable
    indulgent
demanding
    in speech,
scrupulous
    in decorum,
unwilling
    to fail,
    inaccessible
    incessant
    indifferent
    indelible
desiring
    approval,
punctilious
    in household,
restive
    in eros,
    unanswerable
    unbending
    unavoidable
    uncommitted.
I await your reply,
remaining as ever
true to a whim of love
and friendship,

XII

Dear Fortunatus, thank you again for the satire
on Cato's suicide. I have sent in homage some wine
I hope you enjoy. It's from my mother's land in the north
and in good years has proved as amusing and honest
a little wine as to be found in our barbarous climate.
I assume all is well with you since, outside of the verses,
I have otherwise heard nothing. Such is not my case.
Lately, and here I must beg your indulgence, I've doubted
the fitness of my mind or, perhaps, the whole question
of its domain. It's not as if I were visited
by hostile agents or spirits but more a matter of
thoughts, notions, entire flights of fancy arising
from a state as alien to me as Persia. I felt
in those moments my mind hold dominion over me
and not vice versa. I wish to describe a dream
I had one afternoon last week. I'm aware of your
distrust of intuition and even in my current state
I share with you, at least in principle, a certain disdain.
Perhaps, it's the very extravagance of my narrative
I trust will delight you. In any case, let me begin.
I fell to sleep and it was the afternoon of the same day.
I was in a desert though there were a few scraggly oaks
and a crowd of young women as fair as you or I.
We witness a procession of what they call the Chinese,
a small oriental people, with flat features and skin
curiously more yellow than dark. They lead one of their
young men to a scraggly oak and hang him. Apparently,
he had murdered his mistress. When he is dead, his body
is doubled in two, placed as though seated in a deep
but short and narrow grave, without wrappings or arca,
and quickly covered with earth. Instead, his victim is decked
in silk and seated in a litter, borne by four maidens
of the tribe, dressed in white. The procession winds back and forth
over the murderer's grave, as if to crush him down.
We follow these Chinese to a desolate field that appears
to be a burial ground. A round, richly laden table
has been set. The dead woman sits at the place of honor,

on either side her ladies in waiting. The guests then
take their places and begin to eat with hearty appetite.
Between their fingers are two sticks they use rapidly
to pick food into their mouths. Always the dead woman
is served first but, as she never touches anything,
her food is put aside carefully. The meal finished,
the guests rise and withdraw some distance from the table.
Then each comes back, separately and respectfully,
to sit a moment at the right of the guest of honor
and give her such and such advice. All having had their say,
she is put clothed, but without jewels, in a shining
sarcophagus, ornamented with dragons, packed full
of provisions. She is lowered with care into the grave.
Suddenly, all in a chorus bid her a shouting farewell
and she is covered with two feet of earth. They throw on top
the furnishings, jewels, clothes and other objects dear
to the dead woman. Last on this pyre are the dishes
served at her feast. In that arid twilight her maidens
begin to arrange candles and, as one moves forward
to set fire to the heap, I awoke, bathed in sweat. Further
comment seems unnecessary. I await your reply,

XIII

Leucothea,
it is not yet dawn.
Outside my window
the blue hour holds the pool
motionless and dull
as a sick child. Thought
of your scent jails me
as if it were last night
against my skin. This
is the fifth letter
to you I have begun,
not including one tonight
revised in a dream,
of which I recall now
not a single phrase.
I rose moments ago
and went to the window
where in sleep I'd copied
the letter. It is hard
to continue with this.
The wounded, the enraged
persona will not do.
I am none of these.
I am completely and
utterly disappointed.
Leucothea, I peopled
your fiction, your fable
if you will. The moral drawn
there's nothing more for us.
It's been a long, cold
and impossible spring.
I am homesick for the north
where I was young. Yours,
as always,

XIV

Dear Tranquillus, I trust my letter of
last week was not rude in its brevity.
Thinking of our recent evenings together,
I am embarrassed at how amateur
was my deception. I regret having had
to mask the estrangement with Leucothea
but once begun it grew more awkward each time
you and I met. Your dinners became for me
an island, emblematic of the sanity
I had wished to keep apart from the fiction
and bitter disorder of my life. I prefer
to forget how many volleys of yawns lately
you've needed to dislodge me from your table.
I should stop here; there will be time for more.
That my winter's tale had such a feeble end
seems an omen, though of what I'm not sure.
I would like to offer some lines written
after our last evening. The nocturnal float
along the river haunts me still. Perhaps
only fancy driven by my anguish or
there was something else in it, emanating
like a mist of sound from the river itself.

>   Calid midnight on the Tiber,
>   In the still rush the shadows
>   Of voices not ours alone.
>   Our table drifts under nine
>   Bridges echoing with the stops
>   Of eddy and swirl. Caesars'
>   Bridges unlike history
>   Uphold the night as memory
>   And a name and whispers must.

I look forward to another evening with you.
My best to Ludovica, and, as always,
a warm embrace for you both,

XV

Dearest Fabritius,
will your demands on my humor
never stop? I suppose I must
pay you a visit if my
self-pity is to be spared
further laceration. It seems
our Italian climate has been
restored so even that excuse
is unavailable. Caesar
travels hence I sit and scribble,
which, in your mind I'm sure, accounts
more than the unseasonable spring
for my unwillingness to quit
this oasis of marble and
regret. As for Leucothea—
my once winter rose, as you keep
reminding me— I have little
to report. In these last months
I've accompanied her twice
to the theater and otherwise
our lives have had not much to do
with each other. If I may sound
bitter, that's not my intention.
It is more a matter of
so much being behind me now
and wanting to keep it so.
In fact, there's an ease in the
images of self-parody
words like 'desolate' and 'lonely'
inspire— yours truly wind-blown
on headland, rocky shore, promontory,
etc. Only insomnia,
entrenched like a penniless cousin,
demands the sternest of comic
muses— e.g. poet,
moist-eyed, at writing table, bereft
with loss, whispering to himself,

revising line after line
in the chill dawn. His barren,
he would like to think 'chaste,' rhetoric
is for this unsleeping poet
the ultimate proof of candor.
Insomnia, though, is not unrivaled
for the arousing of less than
Olympian taste. Take the case of
a dear friend, courtier, scholar,
sometimes poet, who, venturing
into one of most illustrious
houses of pleasure, found himself
required to mount, before all else,
the winged horse of poesy.
To partially vindicate
these daughters of Aphrodite,
it should be noted that our horseman
had, for his own reasons of the heart,
not visited this or any
of the neighboring sanctuaries
in more than two years. In short,
poetic offerings to the cult,
mostly lugubrious epigrams
in Greek on the passing of time,
became compulsory as silver
and, much to our literate friend's
dismay, equally and endlessly
requested. A brief devotion to
Venus proved arduous as a trek
to Delphi. In any case,
one cannot ignore a clear moral:
that a rich inner life, like virtue,
and even perhaps poetry,
is to be its own reward.
Thus you have, if not the happiest,
the most noble and ridiculous
of friends. Until next I kiss your hands,
I remain, furiously,

XVI

Dear Fortunatus,
if I know what to tell you,
or how to tell it,
or what to leave altogether
untold for the present,
may all the gods
and goddesses in heaven
bring me to an even worse
desiccation than I
now daily suffer.
Did you, dear friend, even
for a moment, assume
this opening were from my pen?
Did the expression,
or perhaps the formal
attitude seem at all
like mine? If you would briefly
indulge me, imagine
I did write such a phrase.
Your critical acumen,
I'm sure, will register
a dozen objections
to my authorship,
not the least of which
might be the extreme
rhetoric, a heightened,
almost obsessive note
of self-awareness
and, more intangible,
a feel of distance
in the language itself.
But haven't you said
similar things of my style,
especially the prose?
I recall almost twenty
years ago, when I first came
to Rome, your comment

on a political essay:
that it sounded written
by a man moments
before his suicide,
embarrassed, disdainful of
mentioning the finality
of his words. And what of
my 'orientalizing,'
as you call my poetry?
Though its composition
is certainly more
musical in purpose,
haven't you there too found
a tortured rhetoric,
a distance and self-concern
as in the opening phrase?
Now, to remove the mask.
The lines I asked you
to consider mine are
Tiberius', from a
letter to the Senate
in which, if I remember
rightly, he refused
the official title,
'Father of His Country.'
The passage is quoted
by our own Tranquillus
in his "Twelve Caesars."
This entire pantomime
sprang from a recent reading
of the manuscript,
after which I asked him
questions like those I posed
to you. Tranquillus
was unequivocal
in his response. Though he might
admit of superficial
resemblances in our styles—
e.g. use of
far-fetched metaphor—
he said my words lack focus,

the historical center
or divinity
of that noble Roman's.
I could not let the matter
drop. I will spare you
the summary of a
whole evening's argument,
except to mention
the initial rebuttal:
that such a focus might be
absent from my writing
because I was born
neither noble nor Roman,
and that he would do well
to look beneath the rubble
of history to avoid
appearing himself
superficial. I
concluded with an offer
of armistice, the main
condition of which
being your judgment
in the matter. I regret
importuning you this way
but my passions and
Tranquillus' excellent
wine outflanked me. I was
clearly losing ground.
Whatever your verdict,
I ask only that your wit
be sharp and heedful
of the muse. Let the hand
of Venus guide yours.
As always, I remain,

XVII

My dear Marcellus, I would be delighted to join
your Festival of Fools. In this 'era of shortages,'
as one of our leading senators pronounced recently,
your idea seems most genial: to honor that pure and
boundless humanity, that ample virtue setting us
apart from god and beast. Indeed it would be rare to find
oneself in the company of somewhat intelligent
persons who did not talk of actors, charioteers,
property values, corn, lumber or oil crises. I should
warn you, by the way, some of us are more than prepared
to be fools. To take a case at hand, a dear friend, trying
to forestall yet another bout with insomnia,
decided to spend a day and night in the city,
and ride back to Tibur early the next morning. He made
a dinner appointment with Gaius Tranquillus and planned
to take his noon meal alone, in an eating house. Our friend
had left the baths and was approaching the Forum when
whom should he meet but one Psyllia, a notorious
African beauty. Though he had not seen her in over
three years, she was as much in bloom as when they first met
ten years before, she barely twenty. She made a great fuss,
calling him 'my eyes, my tongue, my heart,' etc.
To quell the farce to which they treated the passers by,
our friend suggested they might walk together a while.
I should note that Psyllia had been especially fond
of our protagonist. Occupied as she had been
with her profession, she still found time to entertain him
hour after hour. She prized his words in the extreme. She desired
to listen to anything he'd written, whatever
opinions he held, regardless of her ignorance.
If he grew tired or bored, she would take up with stories
of Africa, the witches, the magic, the love potions,
the crimes of passion and, foremost, the loss of her father's
fortune. When she spoke of the four maidservants she had had
to herself as a child, tears would invariably come
to her eyes, soon followed by a rage at all things Roman.
More often than not, her peculiar anger would turn

on our friend. Why did he respect Caesar and believe in him,
and what, she demanded, was our friend doing with her,
when, like his master, he could be slobbering kisses on some boy?
Their relation lasted almost five years, until, required
to spend more time away from Rome, absence became his excuse
to end the affair. With no warning, as our friend followed her
through the mouth of a crowded alley, Psyllia stopped him.
She could restrain herself no longer, she said. She must speak.
The Psyllia he once knew was now dead. She had retired
and bought a villa in Campania and would be settling there
within the month. Our friend, I must tell you, was speechless,
oddly vexed, as he was led the few doors down the alley
to her house. As they entered, she began scolding her maids
to prepare a table fit for a gentleman. He tried
to excuse himself but she would hear none of it. In an hour
our friend was bathed, massaged with perfumed oils and seated
on a pile of rugs, with little, colorful dishes
before him. Psyllia would not stop talking. Her delight
fluttered between retirement and their chance meeting. Her wine
proved quite fortified and even small portions of the
highly spiced food were overpowering. He asked if he could rest.
She told him of course and perhaps she would lie down with him.
When our friend awoke, it was nearly twilight. Psyllia
was asleep on a rug near his bed. As he sat up,
he saw on his legs the writing in purple ink. He read it
and started to shout her name, when Psyllia opened her eyes
and asked if he liked her little gift. He stammered what
passed for a 'yes, certainly,' and that he was already
late for an appointment and had to leave just then. Psyllia
did not object. She simply reminded him of his promise
to return soon. Two hours late by the time he reached the
Palatine, our friend was lucky to find the historian
alone in the garden. There was no time wasted. He launched
into the afternoon's adventure, crowning it with a show
of the inscription: connecting both legs, in a crude hand,
a two-line epigram signed 'Psylli.' Tranquillus was
ecstatic. He placed before our friend a bundle of pages
and told him, as fate would have it, he was engaged in his
most inspired work to date, called "Lives of the Famous Whores."
The African's career and that day's episode seemed
indispensable; perhaps they might interview her

tomorrow. Our friend thanked the historian for his good humor
but regretted he could not go along. That morning
he must meet a delegation of architects he'd been
carefully neglecting for over a month. Before he left,
he would write a note to Psyllia and, he assured
Tranquillus, she would be flattered to receive him. And now,
if he might be excused, he would like the ink removed
from his legs. Think of it, said our friend, lying in the
clear bath, pretending to listen to the condescending
logic of the architects, and under their very noses
Psyllia's affidavit:
    Here sleeps the headmaster, three gods in one person,
    Ammon, Apollo and Emperor of my yearning.

                My dear Marcellus,
to make an already long story just a little longer,
no way was found to wash off Psyllia's gift. The next morning,
in fact, accompanied by Tranquillus, our friend returned
to her house. Immediately she had a servant wipe off
the ink with perfumed oils, herself drying the legs with her
thick black hair. Our noble Romans offered their day to her
and to the history of her remarkable career.
Such offering, I hope you will agree, is devout enough
preparation for your festival. I look forward
to your day of Fools, remaining, as always,

XVIII

Dearest, I'm glad we were again able to spend
an evening together. The delight I gain,
no matter how I rage at my fortune,
is undeniable. Again, with fervent and
sweet kisses, you declare me unlike other men,
nor could another, you insist, have nourished
you so. With this last phrase, one I would've thought
impossible only a few months ago,
the trap is sprung once more. But why, you ask,
regurgitate what is only obvious
and painful, why indulge this anguish? If, though,
you would suspend disbelief, you might find my
dire vision, this mortification, as you call it,
something other than self-hatred or pity.
The Jews, in their secret book, have a dictum:
"Man is the language of God." Granted, of course,
one may be disposed to shun their teaching
for its primitive and fanatical
practices. Nonetheless, I consider
this formula to veil a crucial design.
Do some of us, like a statue or poem,
exist unfinished? Whether the artist
loses interest or finds the material or
subject untenable, the result is the same.
The work is abandoned. So it has been
with my life. Whatever was desired most,
I contrived a way to surrender.
My passion for you was the exception.
I could no more surrender you than the self
each day rebuking me, lingering on the face
of these pools like a spoiled dream. Remember
how you would demand I look into the mirror,
how you called me self-indulgent for evading
my eyes. And now that my glance may leer back
at me, what have I learned? In any case,
the question of an unfinished life remains.
I postpone it for now, though I can't expect,
in my fortieth year, to discover

a solution simple or painless as a
shift of the eyes. But, as my mother is fond of
saying, the gods blind us daily with miracles.
Perhaps this letter foretells a change or points
to the obscure passage I must prepare for.
Who can say? Wit, my winter rose, may please you
but it also makes a fine habit for disease.
I await your reply, remaining as always,

XIX

My dear Fabritius, you must know
my respect for the isolate life
you have chosen. I may play
with your sentiments, as with my own,
rename and replace them, color them
as a child would a leaf,
but never bait your friendship.
Perhaps I'm ill at ease not quite
understanding why this is
addressed to you or perhaps
I'm just fond of apologies.
In any case, I pose you, of all men,
a question of husbands and wives.
Last week I had the misfortune of
being invited up to Tibur
for a literary feast.
There arrayed, in the cautious splendor
of my ex-brother-in-law's villa,
was the flower of our capitol.
Even Valerius came.
At one point, he was asked to toast
the wife of a senator
and fellow poet. Whether
the wine in him or what he gauged
to be our stupor, Valerius
began showering verses
harsh as Alpine hail. But that's
another matter. The feast,
apropos husbands and wives,
was a rather insinuated affair—
glances aflutter, erotic
dares flung in the subjunctive,
bolder appetites in the garden.
Two ladies were hard on my scent.
Luckily one was so adamant
in her peevishness at the other's
husband that I conspicuously

served most of the evening
as the table's arbiter.
Of course, the duty fell on me
to accompany both ladies
for a breath of air. You hardly
need imagine how many blooms
and fragrances were sighed over,
how modestly, first one then the other,
steered me into a corner
or under a musky arbor.
Do you detect a wistfulness
in my disdain? It's more and more
repugnant to keep separate
any want of person or thing
from this chronic self-absorption.
Do I wish another wife
like one of those noble ladies?
To put it another way,
could I ever keep a wife,
given what I know of myself
or what I've refused to know
these eight years since my divorce?
There have been others' wives,
with whom for a short while I was
the great swan-necked god himself.
Of course, they were not mine and
might be won or lost, desired or not
with like abandon. For a time
I felt a stranger to myself,
an agent of moonlight on the sea
or river or chamber floor.
I, the would-be god, brought no knowledge
but in her embrace fell to earth
willful as a kite in a dream.
Dear friend, it strikes me that I try you
not so much with questions or
occasions, but with the naive
indifference I uphold. Tonight
a shudder of remorse will tuck me
deeper. The trap is ever more
yielding, consummate. Only what

is incomplete does not seem vain.
I think of Elpenor, first
to break silence in that dim and
breathless house:
   "O my lord, remember me, I pray,
do not abandon me, unwept, unburied..."
You will recall that, unbeknownst
to Odysseus and his crew—
they now ventured into the land
of the dead— Elpenor lies dead
in the world of the living.
I am both Elpenor and Odysseus,
both begging and determined,
you might even say ruthless
to be resolved. Otherwise,
I remain yours as always,

XX

Dearest Fortunatus, I was just awakened
by news of your suicide. Word came from Cinna
via the ubiquitous Melo. The fragrance
of Serapina's trough dominated his lisp.
Damn them all to hell, even if they pervade so!
For a year I've plagued you with talk of suicide.
Now this unseasonably hot morning, the stench
of your mother-in-law's eternal Rome in my heart,
I am face to face with it. Have I become
so morbid and self-absorbed to be mortified
by plain gossip? Or am I just craven
and too attached to the ephemeral circus
I claim to despise? Forgive me. At the moment
I have no courage, only the fury to remain,

XXI

Dear Gorgonius, I forgive
your being an architect.
Of late we've wrangled incessantly
eagles arrayed before even a
word of greeting— astronomy,
physics, geometry, the law,
progress, etc. You maintain
I am retrograde and I
deny your biologic premise.
You quote Ptolemaeus and
the sparkling Leonidas,
while I have eyes only for
the thrush of Lesbos. You think
the divine a naive formula.
I consider man the outrage,
the incapable god. Worst of all, though,
is your damnable Greek platitude—
'technology.' You propose
a new library taller
than the pines or cypresses.
You say Caesar is fascinated.
You insist progress cannot be checked,
the process inevitable
as the design of our bones.
I only remind you of what
was told me late one drunken night,
that we need to build above the trees
because we finally know how.
Is this progress or merely
evolution? Of course, I have
no answer or rebuttal.
Civilization, as ever,
is an adolescent spectacle,
frivolous in its very zeal
to contemporize. I realize
my wit must appear to you
suspect and anything but mature.

But, Gorgonius, tell me this:
in one of your great buildings,
the library, for example,
where will your soul reside? No,
I'm not mocking, if anything
only ridiculing myself.
Surely, you won't try to tell me
your spirit inhabits the design,
bickered over and modified
a hundred times to please Caesar.
Perhaps, like the wily Odysseus
with his marriage bed, you will leave,
in some corner of your edifice,
a small oak in the shape of a
table, where a scholar like myself
may rest a volume or his head.
My soul, incidentally,
is hardly ever where I am.
Caesar calls his a 'charming wanderer,
guest and companion of his flesh.'
Mine too is charming, but almost
never companionable.
I stroll behind at a distance,
like an African bride, glad
to be lost in the afternoon wind,
the clouds that sweep ambition
from my thoughts. Occasionally,
I bribe my little soul with verses
or confession in a letter
scribbled at dawn. Thus, my friend,
I could never trust a monument,
as you do, to translate me
any further than geometry
or the piety of a job well-done.
In this knowledge, I remain,

XXII

My dear son, I hope your service in the north was able
and inconspicuous. These are not distinguished nor
distinguishing times. I trust you visited your grandmother
and bring news of her. When I think of the delicate woman
and how single-handed, while caring for my father,
she has managed to make that land prosper, I'm certain
our devotion to Virgil is grossly misplaced. If we must
have one, our heroic poem should be his Georgics.
I suppose you won't agree but the Roman or, in fact,
the Italian genius is our passion for the earth,
with territory, power and empire a promiscuous
and masculine extension thereof. I insert my notion
of a peninsular identity to remind you
of your heritage and, moreover, to stress an outlook
I find one of the more favorable symptoms of our time.
Unlike your mother, I am not a citizen by birth.
Coming here as a young man, unknown and unprotected,
I would have found much graver obstacles, for example,
in the fabled time of Augustus. Almost daily one hears
how decadent we are, that the rule of Rome has left
the Capitol, that Roman power is in the hands of
a vast and swollen body of provincials. Your father
is of that ripe body, though something on the order of
a pimple or hair. Incidentally the Senate
buzzes about, trying to sting here or there and draw
Caesar's attention: that oriental must be chastened
by the sword, this king has overtaxed the Senate's patience,
the army is in serious disuse, etc.
But with a wave of the hand, their buzzing is ignored
and the body goes about its vast business. Your legions,
though relatively unused, are the most efficient
they have been in fifty years. Without a single triumph
since you were born, Rome has enjoyed a very long peace.
The Emperor chooses to rule not from Rome but from his heart,
crossing the empire on foot with an army of blacksmiths,
carpenters, builders and architects. A vast and swollen body?
A decadence? Perhaps. I only say that there is now

in heart and mind a maturity, a harvest of spirit
that is order not power. Perhaps, as with each mortal
spirit, the harvest may be final, or perhaps,
as with the earth itself, it is indelible.
Hesiod, a millennium ago, called our peninsula
the Island of the Blest, claiming our first rulers were
Agrios and Latinos, borne by Circe in steadfast love
to Odysseus. We are at best a feminine people,
a focus on the affluence and commonplace
of the earth. Here I stop this last in a series
of digressions, noting that it is such views make me,
in your mother's eyes, provincial. Enough. I suppose
you'd like some notice of the mundane. Caesar still travels
so I remain splendidly occupied with nothing
but the occasional administration of delay,
affording me quite a few hours to scribble. I've been busy
a year now on a sizable mosaic of epigrams,
somewhat curious in the mix of Roman and Greek.
I'll send some when I have more confidence in their outcome.
As for what's usually referred to as one's personal life,
I have none. I may spend an evening of wine and argument
with the architect Gorgonius, but otherwise I'm alone
among my duties and my reading and writing. Must I fear
becoming what Fortunatus calls a 'writing machine?'
Or is it in the words of the irrepressible
Strato, 'a consummation devoutly to be wished?'
I look forward to news of your travel and career,
as always, your father,

XXIII

My dear Leucothea,
today begins your twenty-third year
as a citizen of fate and Rome.
I send this thought as omen
of a pleasing and long life:

> Stop with me, admire the pale water at our feet,
> Your face and mine, in a world that is all we are.

It has been, as you know, a year
since we parted, though the fall
of these words would imply more.
I trust my speculations
seem less troubled and encumbered.
As ever, best wishes and
a warm embrace,

XXIV

Dear Marcus, I am aware
you paint every day now and find
no time for wisdom or patience,
though you seem to have leisure
enough for invective. I
do not chide, I stand like you
before my mirror of remorse.
When you were here last to sketch,
you claimed outrage at the world
you have come to inhabit:
greed, stupidity, clamour
and their patrons from here to
Puteoli. Also you complained,
most vigorously if I recall,
of those bountiful matrons
dedicated to the hunt. Thus
the world obliges your pencil
and verifies the solemn title
of 'artist,' in return for
a lifetime of not-too-solemn
obituaries. (In this,
even a patron's ultimate
flattery-- the small lavish
dinner, the remarkable wines,
the witty chatter, the hand
on your shoulder heralding a sigh
of confession that he has often
and secretly wished to change places
in life with you-- is hard nourishment
indeed!) As for the ladies
in this galaxy of refinement,
your rendering leaves me somewhat
uneasy: at forty those
we desire most are either too young
or ambitious to take one
seriously, while those who pursue us
are rather omnivorous,

past their prime or even unstable.
Such categories, however
welcome, seem more than a
little complaisant. Then again,
I am so removed from the hunt
its least incarnation makes me
twitter. As I have said before,
a less morbid wisdom might better
serve us. At fifty, in ten years,
will not this type of matron
still be plentiful and begin
to appear almost enticing?
Would not yet another antagonism
thus be removed and you discover,
with such a companion, a
happier, more productive art?
Of course, it takes a certain patience
to see ten years of one's life
as an accrual of wisdom
and not what, in a more hot-headed
moment, might be perceived as
compromising and submissive.
There you have it, the most sage counsel
I can muster for the New Year.
There is always another road,
though it's rumored to be joyless
and in perpetual disrepair.
However, when you next visit,
we might map this other passage
and warm to its vision with a
jug or two of my mother's wine.
Until then, I remain,

XXV

Fortunatus,
what will you die of?
Has not her indolent smile
altered your indifference?
The virtuous Gorgonius,
even after his heart's
mutiny, plans to drop
with the sparkle of wine
on his tongue. The grape too,
and one last paroxysm
of platitude, will fell
our dear Fabritius.
Marcus, the painter,
longs for the soldier's way
and pictures nothing less
than death on horseback,
in glorious battle,
with his preposterous
sandals laced to the knee.
And the keen impious
Marcellus? He augurs
a wasp or hornet sting
to the scrotum, at the most
intimate of moments,
will turn him to stone.
As lovers, however,
we are insolent
to the sentiments of death,
to that 'night of perfect
sleep.' With Leucothea,
for example, there was
such talk but in a way
which appears, in retrospect,
contrived. What I dreaded
in those moments was not death
but a thing far more cruel:
the loss or waning of love.

There is in love too
a kind of dying,
inevitable as
fleshly corruption,
etc., but let's not
embellish. Perhaps it is
the wrong-headed doubting
north in me (or simply
the absence of love)
but are not the limits
of one's mind in question here,
not psukhe or psyche
or whatever Greek baggage?
As you know all too well,
my pathology thrives:
I, my friend, continue
to die of embarrassment,
daily and irrevocably.
This leads me to wonder,
abruptly I admit,
if you are acquainted with
'Armageddon,' the latest
oriental delicacy
to sour the Capitol.
Transliterated from
the Greek, though apparently
Hebrew in origin,
the word implies final
battle or cataclysm,
in short, the world's end.
(Or am I telling you
what you already know?)
Has Armageddon, then,
arrived in Neapolis?
It may be difficult
to diagnose at first
but you, I am certain,
have the resources.
In my mirror, instead,
I find each morning something
far more distracting and

terrible than the world's end.
Please, keep me informed.
Until then, I remain
necessarily,

XXVI

Dear Fabritius, two weeks ago
at Gorgonius' table, you said
I was cold and without a heart, when I
refused what you all believed (and the senate
acclaimed) a 'national tragedy.'
I do not wish to revive the harsh words
the virtuous architect bestowed on me,
nor your attempts to shout down my objections.
It is not yet a month since the disaster
and already your zeal for that 'rare moment'
and my skepticism both seem far-fetched.
Admittedly, your view of an indifferent
humanity roused by common grief
is a separate issue from Gorgonius'
dogma of progress. Nonetheless, the
whole spectacle remains distasteful
as it was then. I only regret
my untimely dissent may provide fuel
for someone's administrative pyre.
In any case, that I would not admit
tragedy in a shipwreck is not as
callous as you might think. You assume a
definite sympathy between my feelings
and my heart. That is your error. Mine
is in continuing to marvel at this
breach, to exert and, perhaps, indulge it
as I do now. Lately, for example,
it's taken a curious discipline
to admit my longing for a certain friend,
whose wit enthralls me as much as the shape of
her arms or thighs. I plead no delicacy
in discovering myself incapable
of definition. I glow like a schoolboy,
the waters of my bungling purgatory
freshly pink from the visit of desire.
And the silly words come, impetuous
as a farmer's daughter on holiday.

There is, of course, a story behind all this
but it must wait for our next meeting.
Until then, I remind you that few men,
let alone empires, are capable
of tragedy. To falter, to remain
conditional, incomplete is not tragic
but ridiculous, like a twitch of shame
ten years old or signing oneself 'father'
in a letter to a full-grown man one
hardly knows. Failing, the poet sang,
is approved only by flame, fired like clay
to unearth the god within. 'That the trees
have no branches the trunks have no tree'
were his words. More and more they become mine.
As ever, I am your friend,

XVII

Dear Fortunatus,
how should I take the
inscrutable 'You are
luckier than you think?'
Though I would not dismiss
your care, there's a deceit
in my recent letter
I find more urgent.
For several reasons,
not the least of which
decorum, I left the
Emperor out of that
catalog of deathly
postures and avoided
mentioning his return.
Even if I have no desire,
in fact, am loath to account
for his suffering,
it seems unavoidable
(would you say fortunate?)
that I play a part
in these final days.
A little while ago,
for instance, cheeks livid
and purple from the blows
of his nightly protector,
the Emperor crouched
in his bath. He looked up
at no one, seeming
to address the water
in a mild voice. Yes,
my friend, it is my luck
to abide in a daily
pageant, exquisite and
devastating to any
alibi I might devise
for my destruction.

Time does indeed flee
but occasionally spreads
her ample legs to show the
design of humanity.
Until it may be my turn
to stare, I remain,

XXVIII

Dear Mallonia, my greeting,
unlike my affection, is
equivocal. Peculiar,
is it not, how after all these
years I still flounder in the
interrogative. And now,
without our familial harbor,
doesn't speculation bias
even a tender course? Yes, yes,
that impatient and lovely shrug:
the question, then. In writing
Fortunatus I used the phrase
'deathly postures' to recall
a catalog— I'd hoped playful—
of our friends' mortal dispositions.
It's troubled me, however, that
the term should have been 'impostures.'
Undertaking the perfect sleep,
who but a fool or a poet
would carry on being himself?
Does not integrity, then, become
the grand mannerism? Years ago
I heard a Christian preach that
man not only reconciles death
but forges from it a way of life.
In this, aren't we all impostors
before death? Or, for that matter,
my dear Mallonia, in love?
Regardless how he prepares his part,
doesn't the lover find it hard
to believe he is not in love?
Let me put it another way.
Two night ago, for the first time
since the Emperor's return,
I was to spend the evening
away from the Villa. I planned
to visit Tranquillus and ride

back here early the next morning.
On my way up the Palatine,
just after dusk, I was robbed.
I had dismounted on a path
with a splendid view of the city,
and as I led my horse around
a wall, I heard steps behind me.
I felt a blade at my neck.
A voice whispered. Rage thrashed in my skull.
He repeated. He nudged and slid
the blade down my back. Pass behind
the purse, ring and necklace. My hands
would not obey. He nudged again,
the whisper became almost
a hiss. I handed the purse
behind me, the ring, but stopped
with the necklace. Brass, I showed him,
not worth much but my mother's gift.
He tore it from my hand and said
to move away. The blade twitched
as I paused and he almost shouted.
I walked ten slow paces.
I picked up a rock and edged back
along the wall. He was gone.
I looked at the rock I held.
He had sounded young, probably
younger than my son, his speech
from the bowels of the city
where, I suppose, even brass
is worth a meal and bowl of wine.
I had been honest in wanting
to keep my mother's necklace.
He had played by hunger's rules.
I was to bash in his head
to defend my integrity.
So we return, involuted
as the excursion has been,
to the notion of honesty
and imposture and, perhaps,
even affection. What, after all,

could be more earnest than a letter? Inform me, if you would. I am, parenthetically, as ever,

XXIX

My dear Tranquillus, I am only a step
past the salutation and already feel
an ungainly need for apology. Odd
how dwelling on the surface of these hours
irks me. What has failed? The answer, I suppose,
would be false as my question. In any case,
all this to anticipate your request
for the following:
                    the empire of my senses
measures six-foot-one, one hundred eighty-five pounds.
It is forty-one years old. Surviving hair,
dark brown, has partially succumbed to gray.
Complexion is fair and the skin remains
for the most part unwrinkled on the skull.
Bare smooth forehead dominates a boyish oval.
The eyes maintain a stubborn, emphatic brown.
The nose, more aquiline than not, slightly swells
at the bridge. Cheeks are flat and rather common,
but not, as yet, declining to jowls. A bit wide
and narrow-lipped, the mouth seems quick to speak.
Chin is unremarkable, though well-cleft.
Overall, then, we have a long-limbed body
contradicted in a barrel-chested torso
hairier than is today fashionable;
solid enough thighs, adequate calves and
ankles, terminating in large, slim feet of which
the resident of this body appears proud.
As for the impalpable domain, I won't
speculate. What use is another episode
of remorse? Dear friend, I must close. It's almost
dark. There is everything and nothing to do.
Do not worry. I will keep you informed.
Warmest regards to Ludovica, as I
remain affectionately the undersigned,
C. Paullus Lunatus

XXX

Dear son, Publius Aelius Hadrianus is dead.
All is confusion here. Please, do not try to see me.
There will be time soon enough away from the marble
and regret. I suppose most of us convey longing
but here it takes abruptly, the endless blue whispering...
Wait, a shadow passes behind me. It has no name.
Does this outburst embarrass you? Remember four or five
years ago, when you were a very serious student,
my diction was your agony. My, how we mature.
There is a dry wind this morning. It would have pleased him,
blustering west to east, with perhaps the littlest
and dearest of his companions leading that pale fleet.
It is a favorable morning for travel.
Time stretches brisk and sparkling before us. I repeat:
remain where you are. I will be with you, though for now
send only word of my embrace,

XXXI

Dear Gorgonius, I have been several days without sleep,
except now and again dozing in the bath, so you will
allow me some extravagance. For all your deprecation
of what you call my 'little planet' (as if it were
a poorly trained hound), for all your threats to repudiate
mortality, you have, in fact, outlived the Emperor.
May I employ that ill-tempered mirror you have named fact.
Indulge me, please. I would wear your vision like a cloak.
Mine is flimsy and I grow cold. What then of this Villa,
these two-hundred, now certainly unfinished acres?
The republic of dreams vanishes as I scribble,
another evening smouldering on the windy plain,
a shudder soon to be memory, like the first line
of a boy's poem, or the love that staggered one's life
only a year or two before. Yes, time is the perfect
assassin. The leaf is lordly as the tree, the pine needle
impenetrable as this marble it falls upon.
Our Hadrian, a consummate performer, created
the past everywhere he went. He imagined ritual
in his fingers as you would the future. From his marches
across the empire with phalanxes of carpenters,
masons and engineers, to the unending reflections
of this remorseful metropolis, all was a pageant
on the life of the ideal Roman, himself. As much
as you have wished to deny audience, Hadrian
commanded one. What have I been all these years if not
the professional spectator, the chattering mirror
he might adjust with a question, a smile, a few lines
of Greek verse? We have all played our parts, he supremely well.
He let his office and our expectations play through him,
maneuvering even months of pain until the moment
had come for the audience to be released from its terror.
So what of this place and the mobs of shadows that remain?
What of us, may we be spectators without a contestant?
Whose race may we assume? Both of us, however separate
our natures, have invested perhaps too much in our minds.
The Christians and Jews, crude and irrational as their

practices may be, abide fate with a brazen resolve,
one might even say a derision. Surely, it cannot be
subtlety makes them endure. One of their prophets wrote:
"Many times the poet has said to his soul, 'O my love,
I fed the sheep and the little lambs, but when I went to look
for them in their pens, they were torn and bleeding.'" Dear friend,
I have worn your cloak and mine and I still shiver. I will go
inside now and try to sleep. If one's muse is one's destiny,
I remain, uneasily,

XXXII

Dearest, Mallonia, if it is
obviously the lie delights you and
nothing truer than longing
obtains your impeccable grin,
to this engine attach little
but affection and some
eagerness to please. Though wait,
look again at this toy. What
if you were to plead a stubborn
end, to demand spooning from dreams
vast deserts of habit, might you
eventually redeem that
willful innocence for a
heartful of sand? Have you found
a sigh stricter in ecstasy
than pain? Indeed, is this how
your girlishness thrives, the careful
office empowered to the bone, the
uneasy unforgiving heart
holding the mind answerable for
every desire? Is your reason
a daemon then, or a not very
reliable administrator
of the divine? Or have we grown
fastidious in our rage?
My head nods and totters on the
edge of the sentence.
      P.S.
Little is left to finish here.
One's final duties are clear and few.
Vaguely I long to rest, and though I'm
empty, there is nothing more
I dread than waking to a new day.
Suppose I would never close my eyes.
Very few things pertain except the
abruptness of silence in a world of
solutions. We will talk soon, until
then I think drowsily of you,

XXXIII

My dear Fabritius, the summer should be full
upon us but for now mercifully relents.
To have ended so in the heat seems ignoble.
Less than an hour ago I woke from my first sleep
in almost a week. My carcass at the moment
is imbued with a certain equilibrium and clarity.
This was to have been one of those epistles
that would tell all-- in a fit of mawkishness
I even considered asking you to circulate this
among several friends. Don't fear, sleep
has spared you any such duty or embarrassment.
By the way, have you noticed my letters to you
inevitably contain some talk of the weather?
I'm sure you will give this fact the inattention
it deserves. In any case, it is your exile
from concerns that pinch my thoughts and render me
the most disdainful of spectators makes
what I am about to say almost appropriate.
This past winter I decided to astound you
(and, most unfortunately, myself) with larceny.
I would close out my days as the person you had known
embezzling the empire. I've considered other
death masks but find them much too morbid
for the ridiculous journey I'm about to undergo.
You will remember in my most difficult time
I envisioned suicide as a sacramental gesture,
redeeming all the chatter, the unfinished life.
You were then, as I'm sure you would be now,
relentless in your deflation of what you called
my 'principles.' My stance seemed histrionic.
You wouldn't concede how death belongs
to anyone but oneself. Dearest Fabritius,
I am awash in more than bath water.
The time for weather reports is done.
The razor and cream sit in the dish.
I will summon your favorite, Ascyltus, to carry
this letter. Then I will shave with pleasure

and, I trust, be done with that remorseful device.
I will dress in my best tunic and boots
and mount the stallion I'd requested before
stepping into the bath. My direction will be north.
My soul will have gone on far ahead.
My heart, I had meant to say, would be left
in this bath but instead stops in the memory
of kissing your brow,

Alephs Again
[1988-1989]
1999

for Adriano Spatola (1941-1988)

A is an angel who wants absolutely nothing. She looks elegant in torn trousers and almost never answers the phone. She seldom speaks, especially when spoken to. Right now A's on Adriano's lap making him laugh.

B is bothersome, even bitter sometimes, when substituted for the first letter of your name. Not B, you say, aping your father, V as in victory. Both of you lack ambition.

C is a constant, not unlike chance or a comma not critically needed, or a capital after a colon or after so many days and nights and letters and intercontinental calls and an ecstacy still of exclamations. C definitely lacks charity.

D is for deeds done and undone as in legend or democracy, for instance, which you may truly love in order to destroy. Without T there isn't any D. Ideologically speaking D is always hard.

E is easily the most equivocal letter in many European languages. A dipping of the tongue past expectation. Especially when it's become the first letter of your name.

F is found frequently in Finland where I'm told the major golf tournament tees off at midnight June 21. Or is it Iceland? Fortunately none of us needs to find out.

G is the most generous letter in the gnostic alphabet. Gregarious to the extreme, he gets under his lover's skin by generally preferring an evening around the table with friends to her whispered generalizations. G also likes good shoes.

H, like hopelessness or history, is happily absent from this alphabet. He's high-minded and writes criticism. H, like heart, is a commodity.

I is for the innocence I won't insist upon. I remember stopping a little boy or girl on the street, or marching into the butcher shop under our apartment to give away my favorite toy. Often something I'd pestered my mother about for weeks. I tried to write an entire book once without I.

K is king in the knowledge that a kingdom demands the killing of its sovereign. Or else K is tired of waiting in the Caffé Canova, watching two elderly German ladies consume a plateful of sandwiches they told the waiter they didn't care for. K is a great kidder, if sometimes a little unkind.

L lingers from the other alphabet, a platitude abandoned, a leak from the other side. L wants nobody except maybe some angels, Uncle Bob, his son, T, and his daughter, S, I who got married and seldom talks to on the telephone and now and again a few dead friends. L certainly never felt good about himself.

M means all that has mattered, whom you've loved and left out of this alphabet. M's also the man you will never be. Oh well.

N isn't for the novel not written, not those poems Nevin would never show me. N is a hero who knocks out the eye of the monster and beholds a long-legged Nausicaa orient among the waves.

O, incidentally, has no private life, what others call a 'life of one's own.' From the desk O sees a little man operate a power mower for a minute or so up and down a patch of lawn. Soon O's tall blond neighbor, in red shoes as usual, occupies the street with her stride. O is pleased.

P is for politics, the art of pretending to have some power over life. Others are necessary to play. All are expected to have plenty of persistence, some ambition and a winning pleasure. The dead are no good at it. Only children are ill-prepared for politics, until they produce families of their own. Particularly when they think they need to be loved.

Q is unquestionably the queerest letter in the alphabet. When's the last time, for instance, you quoted somebody from Quito? Maybe my tall blond neighbor, who's Spanish-speaking, is from Ecuador. That would qualify her disdain.

R seems always reasonable. Even when he's never eaten there before. Recently, he tends to make a strong impression. But who knows? Life's irregular that way. At 3:38 this morning a rather strong earthquake kept R awake almost an hour waiting for the aftershock. Which of us, after all, can truly rise to the occasion?

Somebody said S is the most overused sound in poetry. I lisped as a boy so they slit the fraenum under my tongue and sent me to speech lessons on Saturdays. Even if the face of the earth shook, how soon and sentimental depends on the depth of the quake. It seems hard to consider any name but Simone for my daughter.

T is temporarily charismatic, a capital of tenderness. Above it teeter all the excuses you've ever invented. T makes you do things you daren't because there might not be another time. T is the letter, amid a whisper of dashes, the man upstairs most regrets. T plays the odds. T always takes time. T is one of my son's names.

Unless U is unquenchable rich men will unearth the kingdom of heaven. He sees a fat boy urge a foot off the curb to scurry across the street under his mother's eye. U as usual feels unfulfilled when he's more likely undone. He's never yelled, "Kill the umpire!"

Very little varies. Vain resentment then some vague acceptance of a vainglorious life. So much for verisimilitude or the Uncle Fred you were threatened with too virulently becoming. No longer the victorious V coached by your dad, the fervor of the almost bitten lip, but now come south to lazy empire, the late vowels and the weakened stops, where not only all the ladders start but your name too, as in bad, bag, band, bang and bank.

W's always been a mystery. The complement of mother or a waltz in the waves. Either way sounds windy and not much to do with women or writing. Little's got to do with writing. Maybe whiskey, maybe not.

X is too imposing for words. There's only one under X in my thesaurus, X-shaped, and that too chiasmal.

Y I've always heard as a question: whether in the female attitude just yielding enough or upside down standing as a man in all too simple yearning. The Greek *i* it's called in Italian. Yes is, in fact, more like it.

Z is much closer to the start than you ever imagined. She stands apart, on nobody's lap. If anything you'd love to lay your bitter head on hers. If she speaks it's right out of the top of her forehead. Or so it seems. Z, not X, marks the spot.

The Book of Life
[1989-1991]

Book I

In the coming world, say the Hasidim, all will be furnished as it is here. As the room is now, so will it be then. Where your child now sleeps, there also will it sleep. Everything will be as it is, only a little bit different. In hell our reporter finds Increase Mather, Milford, Connecticut, the Beatles, Sam Goldwyn, Louis B. Mayer, Charlie Chaplin, Adolph Hitler, Harvard College, United Artists, the 13 Original Colonies, lots of angels and real estate and many of the people he knows. In hell the phone rings often.

1

Angels are privileged in name only.
There and there and there.
Even pouting at the microphone
listen to her big feet.
In the First Article We Ask:
Is the Book of Life a Created Thing?
Like a paper wing or pine needle on glass
a book is for someone to read.
Angels are lost easy, especially in the rain
or if you leave three shirts out on the line
one more day because they sounded good.
A thing's different in a mirror and in a book.
Are married angels especially misnamed?
Listen to the book, a mouth plays the same.

2

Vaseline. What's it doing in a thesaurus?
Books copied from the original are called books
even the minds of men and angels.
n. Petrolatum (*British*). That's funny.
Who's ever heard of angels in the rain?
Or rhetorical snow.
As the conductor was warned in Boston
for reciting poems to commuters.
'The rhetoric of snow' actually,
by Mary Somebody. Passengers loved it,
the radio said. How would I,
thinking of angels or if married angels,
not to mention veritable snow?
Vaseline. Listen.

3

A poet told me she got the fear of commas
in her mother's womb. That's funny.
That letters in a book differ from the pages
on which they are written is a defect of books.
Can angels have babies or only in the rain?
Crows, I read, take devilish intelligence
and like to misbehave; though they be lost souls
and easy or not to listen to
and often make me laugh. Not so with angels.
'In the head of the book it is written...'
What's the first word in your thesaurus?
Abandon's mine. Seems cold
without sox on after the rain.
Space, *n.* 1. *See* Time.

4

In every book writing is other than the book.
The table in the morning is deep green
often with branches wiggling in it.
Try to remember something in the night.
Butterflies everywhere,
even ones friends tell you are moths.
That's funny. You are traveling with her
pausing at a hotel or in somebody's house.
The minds of angels can also be called books,
even though what's written in them is unclear.
So? Unlike real life she's late, coming peeved
or with absolutely the wrong person.
A scream happens most often in another part.
8. The reply is clear from what has been said.

5

How many pecks would a woodpecker?
Almost three weeks since any hummingbird.
In my son's old room on the floor
are two rows of collages of angels
on 8 1/2 x 11 sheets of ply.
And an even greater distance
is between him an a written word
signifying the word within his heart.
So? Since the three weeks in the garage
slicing pasting bleaching lacquering sanding,
no what? There are more butterflies around
than one would pretend. The scream, it should be clear,
is what you sometimes have to to wake up.
So the book of life is predicated personally.

6

Love is a closet turned off and on.
Hummingbird still away though the air is teeming
with others. Mostly white moths, bumblebees,
crows and mockers. We concede the fifth argument.
Palms on bright fog and a pale two-and-a-half
skyscrapers beyond. That's not funny.
A mother leads her chubby boy uphill.
He chatters at her behind and runs ahead.
Otherwise God, who is called a lion,
would have to have claws and a mane.
This morning gardeners are everywhere.
O the blowers, O the pickups rolling downhill.
The phone rings: Mom from San Francisco wondering
if I did my taxes. Isn't that funny?

7

Procession from a writer is not implied by *book*
anymore than procession from a builder
is implied by *house*. That is funny,
sooner or later. Cooking a cauliflower
for lunch. A mustard sauce maybe and a bottle
of French rosé outside under the cedar.
There's a nice breeze, anyway. Half bottle
of vodka and beer will have to do.
Call D for an appointment for E and me.
Says all is well though up this morning
with what feels like some sort of virus.
Vaseline. A woman at a party wondered
if I didn't have a good thesaurus.
She was sweet but no angel. That's not funny.

8

Question eight: the Intelligence of Angels.
Someone, not in jogging clothes I think,
just ran downhill fast. So seem the cars.
And two fire engines. Even the white moths.
It was a motel in my sleep, she a drowsy
seraphim sang vocals in a rock band.
Floated off for a bottle of scotch and
couldn't find her or her room when I came back.
All those same blue doors with brass numbers.
All the wrong people writhing behind them.
A woman whom I awakened helped with the doors.
They were unlocked. She didn't knock.
She knew where Becky, my angel, would be.
I said keep the scotch, I got a flight.

9

In the First Article We Ask:
Do Angels See God Through His Essence?
Friday night's chez moi were a start.
Though seldom an angel and mostly the boys
who ate and drank glorious disputation
long into the night. As it regarded baguette
in the urinal, a full year passed until
the final cause was furnished by Genet,
via E, whom he (E) had run into
in the men's room of a Paris air terminal.
According to John: "No man hath seen God
at any time." Commenting, Chrysostom writes:
"Not even the heavenly essences themselves,
I mean the cherubim and the seraphim."

10

A hand in a pail of rum. A manual
of providence and hunger for audience,
I admit, palms forefront even now.
The apparent junction of earth and sky.
The hands were chopped off and sent to Boston,
arriving the same day. Record 100 degrees
yesterday, April 4. While the Chief's head
was carried in triumph to Plymouth
where it stuck on a pike twenty years,
a favorite nesting place for wrens, and in time
Increase Mather delightedly carried away
the jawbone of 'that blasphemous leviathan.'
Hand in a pail of rum, sloshing up and down
the provinces. Vaseline.

11

Aren't angels better left to angels?
Bouzouki. A twanging Greek instrument.
A hard question or rather one almost
impossible without having it show.
Urging, that is, an answer and her mouth.
Ginsberg: 'Poetry is the head of a dead cat.'
Obliging that once, in the province
of North Beach after a year of college
or Sunset Boulevard pushing a cab
toward midnight of 1972?
If one weren't allergic to cats or angels
or have them both to watch out this window
much of the time. Hand in a pale of rum.
Horizon. Of an urgent mouth.

12

'Shakespeare has done more to kill poetry
than the mockingbird.' Uncle B,
who isn't running for President in '92
since he just won a poetry fellowship
and will trust the $5,000 in the bank
rather than the public mind. *Praise be
to Christ and all Creatures here Below.*
Mendelssohn, on Uncle B's turntable
one sort of kick starts by spinning a few times.
Piano Trio #2, Opus 66.
A pale. A punctured mind. Provident
if impenitent here below.
'Bare ruined choirs where late the sweet birds sang.'
Of earth and sky and forgiving mouth.

13

Voted: Milford, Connecticut, 1640:
that the earth is the Lord's and the fulness thereof.
Another record, 105 yesterday.
Jack Spicer to Ferlinghetti, March '64:
"You will probably be puzzled by this letter
(explicit as it is) as you have been by my isolated
(the words individual and idiotic come to mind
having exactly the same meaning at root)
attempt to boycott your bookstore. I thought, and still think,
paperback culture, things picked and published
for their currentness, was replacing the library
(the Public Library, remember?) and not much different
in its effect and cause than the Beatle Records.
It was, and is, worse— a company store."

14

Voted, that the earth is given to the Saints.
More Jack to Ferlinghetti: "The enemy
is in your own country, Rosa Luxembourg said
and she, poor dead things, was as unsuccessful
revolutionary as I have been.
My own country is poetry—
and the singlehanded revolution
I attempted was about as intelligent
as assassinating President McKinley.
There are presidents (many of them)
that come after him and will be worse."
Are books and mirrors better left to books
and mirrors and death and sky here below?
Vaseline. Apparently an unction of saints.

15

Voted, that we are the Saints. Connecticut,
Milford. Vaseline. 1640.
All around the mouth, here and there,
watch the world turn. *Word,* it's been said,
implies a real procession whereas *book*
implies procession only according to
a way of understanding. Often as a verb
it takes a T-shirt, billboard, dildo, etc.
Or a stretch of blue behind an airplane
or a heart-shaped cloud on the face of rum.
Unless, on the contrary, we name god
only from things that exist here below.
On a day too rainy for most angels
in Massachusetts or Connecticut.

16

A stench of blue behind an airplane.
As in Los Angeles London Paris Rome.
O bury me not. A small heart-stopping world
once thought to be what a mouth was about.
Everything strives to define itself
and thus perish behind a pail of rum.
The deer and the antelope definitely
long to roam over questions of. The sex
of angels, for instance? Roam, roamed, rum.
Maybe too the ecstasy of double
suicides after a night of no or yes.
Bouzouki. The hanging Greek instrument.
The errant junction of earth and sky,
palms foreground and the rest inurgently pale.

17

The infinite hand we have for rum.
That's not funny, except in Hadrian's reign
when water consumption almost doubles in Rome.
I'd written *for love*, though that was years ago
when we were married and happy and
had much less of a sense of humor.
The hummingbirds are still gone.
What's keeping them? Everyone has ideas:
from the heat fermenting their sugar water
to a recent family of squirrels.
Nobody is considering angels
and the upswing in their activity.
Heat's finally broken and the birds louder.
Who can tell in the rain, sulky or not?

18

I never knew fear until I kissed Becky.
Be bop de beep. Spring can really.
With lots of hair and big brown eyes
just an angel in disguise. As what?
Fresh sugar water in the feeder
after the last batch was ten days untouched.
Still no hummingbird. An angel's gender
appears at best bright or rhetorical.
'And the Lord spoke to Moses face to face,'
while the gloss reads, 'No man, no angel
has ever seen the essence of God as it is.'
Instead are married angels or babies
especially in the rain? There now—
a few seconds, the first in almost a month.

19

Bird at the feeder only that once.
Like a little prayer no end and no beginning.
Unlike men are angels part of nature,
you know, one oar in Eden? Or not.
At the market on the cover of *TV Guide*
Joan Collins says, 'I'm no angel.' Bouzouki.
Missed being by thirty years. Maybe the daughter
she doesn't have. Or that day in '59
she can't remember, when R and I saw her
in some western at the Esquire on Market St.,
underwater and at least twice under a sheet.
We are very quiet on the bus home
and don't even transfer as usual
to a cable car. Oh well. Be bop de beep.

20

Angels is how man reads God. Bazooka.
In the fridge in the kitchen downstairs
he turns the lightie on. Feels like flying.
He loves to sleep or cook or write in the rain.
November 23 and April 12
A and A dead of the heart.
O the morality of rain
O the infamy of drainpipes.
In less than five months. Be bop de beep.
The air is asleep, cowboys weep,
mockers hot as pistols this pale morning.
At what time can workers legally start
in a residential area? Flitting
branch to willow to palm to No Parking sign.

21

At least twice in the last half-hour or so
hummingbird has been at the feeder.
Seventy-one years of oxygen
is all we have left, doctor told N
who yesterday told me when I asked
if he wanted children. Perhaps you would want
to manage your pregnancy differently,
doctor said to L and J before testing
for birth defects. Be bop de beep,
the Indians went to sleep with the birds.
Do wop de bop, in the fridge in the kitchen
downstairs who turns the lightie on?
De beep de bop, angels have one oar in Eden
the other in a pail of rum or not.

22

What Are the Four Intelligent Creatures?
Chinese have no man on the list, I guess,
since who needs brains most of the time.
Fresh sugar water is in the feeder
though no birds yet. Dogs I might have thought
but the Chinese roast them and are after all
too loyal to be thought intelligent
unlike cats. Or is there a problem
of translation with the term 'creature'
if no birds come? Though plenty of white moths
and mockingbirds hotly in song.
Shakespeare. Bazooka. Feels like flying or
dying maybe. They are: the Unicorn,
the Phoenix, the Tortoise and the Dragon.

23

Windows on two sides of me are critical.
Communists and beatniks have little to do
with each other except in the minds
of JH and Samuel Goldwyn.
Be bop de beep. Who've always had a thumb
on the pulse of Indiana. Two walls of windows
here above. And a childhood full of dragons,
paper and otherwise, didn't sound broadening
at the time. De wop de bop. Stop the bus
and let my brother Jack.
Quando Amor ditta dentro. Whose Jack?
The birds are still as someone drills next door.
When love brought in all those *s*'s.
That Jack whose love ate the red wheelbarrow.

24

Quando il cor ditta dentro. Last week
the heart brought in Antonio and Sugar Ray
140 days after Adriano.
Fighting weight. Paper wasn't sure of
Robinson's age, at least 67
it said. Antonio was 54,
Adriano 47 when the heart
wanted in. Sugar Ray was the coolest
dragon of my childhood, pound for pound.
JH did a fine poem of a boy
on a Bronx street on one knee fielding
when RR's fuchsia Cadillac convertible
turned the corner like a rainbow.
Listen to her big feet.

25

That's for the birds, mother likes to say.
Like the 100th birthdays this week
of Charlie Chaplin and Adolf Hitler.
Charlie, astonished more by angels than marches,
built Tudor cottages on Poinsettia Place
to billet all of his. Adolf went in
for Broadway, Wagner and Busby Berkeley.
Charlie liked them young and naughty
or naughty and young. United Artists.
Sloshing up and down the provinces.
Be bop de beep. Hath murdered sleep.
Just when the heart wanted in. There.
An angel flits downhill crouched over handlebars.
A pale, a punctured mind, in purple and white.

26

Still no hummingbird since last Monday.
Gusty northwest winds.
Butterflies in the air like paper.
Sugar Ray, Adriano and Antonio
were none of the names they were born with.
Walker Smith begot Ray Robinson,
Leo Paolazzi Antonio Porta
and Bruno Spatola had Adriano
by heart. I wonder
if poets wouldn't study meteorology.
Might give the winds and else to think about.
Especially those of us from San Francisco.
Paper wings and dancers.
Adolf and Charlie and names we are born with.

27

Buy heart. Wind's up even stronger today.
Everything quick and bright like childhood.
All those *s*'s, if the heart wanted in.
That is, how it used to be in childhood
considering the wind. Be bop de beep.
My tall blond neighbor from Ecuador's
not wearing any red, not even heels.
No hummingbird in a week or so.
Who Killed Poetry? as the magazine says.
Listen to her big feet. By heart.
Lordly men are to earth o'ergiven.
Beyond the pale of rum. Consequently
the book of life doesn't mean anything
uncreated. When the heart wants in.

28

Citizens of Beauty, Jean Senac's title,
who was murdered for having it in men
instead of angels. Today light and dark,
northwest winds, clouds looming after.
'Gasoline, comrades, gasoline!' wrote Senac
about false revolution. Winds gusting
white and black, chimes steady as mockingbirds.
'Poetry is nothing but an attempt to escape
death— *stop*— that's why death is so vindictive
vis a vis the poets it watches for them
everywhere— *stop*— said Yevtushenko
in a telegram when Senac was stuffed
in a pail of rum. 'Farewell, brothers,'
said Senac, 'and we could have loved one another.'

29

Bazooka. The dangling Greek instrument— *stop*
'But tragic as the death of the poet may be
it's not as terrible as if death attacked him
from the inside— *stop*— the internal death
kills even the memory of the poet— *stop*—
and if another world exists I hope Jean
is looking at us with his helpless eyes
and wishing us not to die from the inside.'
Moscow-Algiers, October 1973.
Still cloudy, blowing white and black.
Birds kind of quiet especially
with the washing machine. A book exists
for someone to read on. Balck and white
and far away. Vaseline, comrades, vaseline.

30

The clouds have not moved since yesterday.
Traffic seems to be getting faster or.
Especially as I use especially so much.
So? Who snaps the lightie on? If no fridge,
no kitchen downstairs, and No Parking
Any Time across the street. Bouzouki.
Lots of bees, though, in the hydrangea.
Do wop de bop. I didn't know what time it was.
K stopping by to see how my garden grows.
T's to be here at 1.
F just sent me *My Uncle Joseph Stalin*
by Budu Svanidze (Putnam, 1953).
My favorite chapter so far
is "Uncle Joe's Wedding." Georgia, Georgia.

31

K recalls the day in Poland Uncle Joe died
a kid in third grade jumped up and sang,
*Long live Father Stalin and his mouth
sweeter than raspberries.* In a pail of rum.
GH says Monk is a real angel
and named his sons Wilder and Aeryl.
On the funny side of the street
a gardener shepherds leaves with a blower.
Up the hill another yanks his on.
Who ever thought you would listen to this
instead of sonnets or mockingbirds?
Simple ain't easy, H says that Monk said.
All those *s*'s. The gardeners quit blowing.
The mockingbirds sound much longer now.

32

Somebody said I have everything at this window.
Don't ask who. We both might be embarrassed.
Be bop de beep. Who is that tall gray man
that you'd admit to? A pale, a punctured palm
at the end of the mind pretty to look at?
Above a clack a high noon is.
Evenhanded or not, here they come.
This is clear from the Apocalypse:
And the books were opened— which Augustine
explains as meaning the hearts of the just.
De beep de bop. A palm's nothing to sneeze at,
nor a hummingbird. Will try one last feeder
of red sugar water. In this sense,
what is more common is more noble.

Angels are not evenhanded or else.
It's late Sunday morning and everyone's
on their way to brunch and look at houses.
Who would please finish the sentence about angels?
The Father is the head of the book.
Tell my son that. He might believe it
if he hadn't enlisted in the Coast Guard.
Look at me. Odd way to open a song.
Or else the belly-up of the singular.
My son tells me they are not often belly up
when they pop to the surface. Be bop de beep.
They are all asleep from sea to shining.
Traffic is looking up and down the stupid.
The business of Sundays is Sunday.

Book II

Purgatory is crowded: Fats Waller, Joseph Stalin, Geoffrey Chaucer, T.E. Lawrence, Charles Ives, Lollipop & Falstaff, Verna & Trixie, Horace Walpole, Peter Whigham, Cesar Vallejo, Bud Powell, San Bernardino, Ludwig Beethoven, Charles Baudelaire, Dante Alighieri, C.P. Cavafy, Venus, Pasiphae, Walter Benjamin, William and Georgia Yeats, Jack Spicer, the Lenin Shipyard, Adriano Spatola, Antonio Porta, Sugar Ray Robinson, Helmut Maria Soik, Vladimir Mayakosky, Henry Wadsworth Longfellow, more Harvard, more real estate and more angels. Many of his friends and acquaintances are there too. In purgatory our reporter screens his calls.

1

Hummingbird back at the end of the mind already four times and not yet eight o'clock.
"Angels are not easy to quiet," the half-Algerian actress read, "but human beings are more difficult."
Traffic down and up.
Nothing otherwise in the air or glass but bird twitter.
Look at me.
Is that funny?
While somewhere up the hill it's Thursday and a garbage truck every so often bangs a load.
Be bop de beep.
I think she has it backwards about angels.
Your pedal extremities are colossal, sings Fats Waller at the feet of.

2

Joseph Stalin Entering Heaven.
Charles Ives could have never written that music.
He was only 80 when he died.
"Yes, and what brought Columbus to New York?" said T.E. Lawrence lifting his fork.
Better left to Uncle Joe's nephew, Budu, who was much older when he was born.
Almost 9 in fact.
I tire myself seeking an epithet for the mockingbird till the garbage truck rounds the corner and I rush to greet him with a wastebasket full of bills.
Mad at you 'cause your feet's too big, warbles Fats.

3

Again: a thing is more susceptible to being heated the less that it requires to become hot.
Traffic and birds loud and who on my answering machine can't find the keys.
I didn't know what time it was.
Or as the botanist on the radio observed of the ecology of fire:
"The heart is seldom a good listener."
Hummingbird steady at the feeder.
Coffee mug leads me like a lantern through my days.
P at his car with an African walking stick.
Backwards, she has it, about angles.
For example, a stone is not the form of any matter.

4

P was by with Yellow Crayon, color he's painting his study.
Right ankle itches with three spider bites.
Intellect is stronger when it knows than the will when it loves.
Do wop de bop.
Jay tout perdu mon temps et mon labour, sang Fats at the front of the bus in that empty city.
Look at me.
That's only funny especially.
Consequently, Augustine says, intellect goes first, heart follows after or not at all.
Lollipop doesn't lick is a dog that's not trained to.
Falstaff, her brother, Uncle B has often told me, is.

5

Four years because his shoes were size 11.
So began Stalin's last deportation to Siberia in 1913.
De beep de bop.
Though even in an evening gown with cane, on the arm of a member of
    Parliament, Uncle Joe had big feet.
Listen to her.
Are they not all angels sent forth to serve?
As Trixie held him down on his Donghia laminated table, Verna pulled down her
    pants and laid several soft farts in his face.
I didn't know what time it was.
Hummingbirds back to almost a feeder a week.
Cedar boughs nod in glass.
For it was not for angels that He made the world to come.

6

And: Thou didst make Him for a little while lower than the angels.
Saturday, Memorial Day weekend.
Thou and Him.
Slower than the angels nobody is driving down or up.
Your Ugly, stenciled all over New York, H tells me on the phone yesterday.
Must be a rock band, she says.
Or a band of theologians I think but don't ask in no mood to make her laugh.
Your Ugly.
A pronoun soon to be all over Los Angeles.
Darkness, says Dionysius, is in god because of the abundance of his brightness.
Or vice versa?
Listen to her.

7

Where de man wit de hammer gone?
Baby Born to Brain Dead Teenager in San Bernardino.
Where Uncle Jack says modern poetry turned when Yeats chatted with the shades
    on the Southern Pacific rattling toward L.A. on his honeymoon.
Stalin had a little workshop in the Kremlin, writes nephew, Budu, where he fixed
    Nadja's shoes.
As his wife Georgia was in a trance, Uncle Willie put a question to the spooks:
What are you here for?
It was while he repaired a pair of her summer sandals that Uncle Joe shaped the
    theory of the possibility of socialism in a single country.

8

Where de man wit de hammer?
Two pigeons wobble down the slope of the gray roof.
In the first we judge how a thing should be, a judgment made by a superior
    about what is inferior.
Gone, children, look behind the door.
In the second we judge how things are.
Hummingbird twitter high in the tree guards the feeder.
And this judgment can be both about what is superior and what is equal.
Or, as Jack says the spooks sung to Uncle Willie:
What is more permanent and common is more noble.
For we are equally able to judge who is standing or sitting, whether he be a king
    or peasant.

9

I know what I see from the window.
There and there.
Listen to her big feet especially.
Walter Benjamin too had it wrong about angels, all those symbols agonizing the line.
Angels are here like lemons or skyscrapers in the June fog.
Where Walter's passion really was was in books, collecting them especially.
His Angelus astute as something you'd hear at Harvard at the beginning of the term.
Do wop de bop.
When angels haven't yet been put to sleep with the Indians.
"Ownership is the most profound relationship one can have with objects," says Walter.

10

What I see from the window is a red slipper in a door and a man with a black ponytail, a cigarette in his lips and two white shopping bags stroll downhill.
"Every passion borders on the chaotic," Benjamin writes, "but the collector's passion borders on the chaos of memories."
Backwards too about passion.
I never knew what time it was.
The birds do as do angels though you can't always know by listening.
Most of us sing by the clock sooner or later.
Sometimes a mockingbird sits on the aerial and jumps up and down in the wind.
Be bop de beep.
Don't gossip, warned Mayakovsky after his death.

11

The mockingbird at his dance a couple of feet in the air every ten seconds or so
    and floating back down.
Even on a cloudy Sunday morning, the first of June.
Everybody so busy.
A man is walking three dogs uphill.
Four dark copters in formation slide behind the skyscrapers at the horizon.
I tell K when he phones who says they're probably just shooting a movie.
Two couples in black Mercedeses call on the little flags in front of the house for
    sale across the street.
If it were elsewhere these clouds might be bringing rain.
And fire.

12

'He needs must obey when the Angels says, write!'
Longfellow who didn't need any help with his.
Uncle Joe's watering can was painted orange.
Jose's couldn't see through the widow.
It's five Sunday afternoon, Open House signs and little orange flags have been
    put away.
Other things a tall woman in black deposited in the trunk of her long black car
    but then those, unlike angels, are not visions to stake a life on.
Maybe I might mention the objectivity of poems separated from readers.
Maybe I ought to rise and go now take a piss.
His favorite color.
From my window.
Before the sea again closes over.

13

"Nay, I already say my alphabet of six colors, and know each stands indiscriminately *but* for four letters, which gives the Peruvian a great advantage over the Hebrew tongue, in which the total want of vowels left every word at the mercy of the reader; and, though our salvation depended upon it, we did not know precisely what any word signified, till the invention of points, which were not used till the language had been obsolete for some thousands of years."
In the wild wild west.
Horace Walpole, 1781.

14

Prove all evils.
GH says on the tape of that obsolete city.
De beep de bop.
Someday we'll make a solar man,
says Uncle Joe tending his flower garden of turtledove gray roses and black tulips.
That's only fun eventually.
Or when love is spelled backwards.
And this said by Uncle Joe to his nephew only a couple days before they went fishing on a Sunday morning in June on the Black Sea as Hitler's troops sublimated Russia.
To cough where the dream never did.
Stalin had two fish on, a kambala and a five pound kefal, when he got the news.

15

To see what I know from the window is bad theology but good business.
Instead of I know what I see from the window.
Which never turns a dime on Wall Street though it has kept angels at one's door.
K calls to say the widow of Johnson's Wax bought the Lenin Shipyard in Gdansk.
Be bop de beep.
Yellow jacket's at the sugar water in the feeder.
June 6 though my feet are cold without sox.
To dream where the cough never did or not.
K also says something about Frank Zappa in business as a trade consultant to
    Russia before the sea again forecloses.

16

Love is a college turned off and on.
Many need help with their Longfellow or else.
How much can you conjugate in English?
Especially beyond a pale of rum.
The dead are wonderful, says Uncle B.
Meaning, I suppose, their vision if not their perfect manners.
Nobody wants the floor.
Everybody ate his dumb turn.
A similar reply should be given to the second, third and fourth difficulties.
Mockingbird that keeps floating in the air and flapping down, what kind of soul
    is he?
The dead start where the dream never did, and you?

17

Ivy at the shore— somebody's title.
And a small signal of how the bird on the aerial does in fact sound.
On a postcard unsent, unsigned under a front tire yesterday.
Almost noon though the traffic still seems vast.
Oh well.
People with briefcases visit the man up the street every day now.
A little sign.
Assimilation is required for this reason only.
A sparrow doesn't stay a minute on the aerial.
So that the knower be in some way united to what is known.
All those *s*'s the dream never does.

18

Barely two-and-a-half skyscrapers beyond.
Fog turned to mist in the night is fog again.
Done with the compass.
Done with the heart.
If only I could find one in spite of all those *s*'s.
De beep de bop.
Dream of talking to a doctor on the phone in San Francisco of my son dying.
(No exceptions in the literature, Doc said.)
wouldn't give my back to sleep.
Sage sparrow's song of 4-7 high thin notes (third note highest)
folds my hands on the desk to listen.
Doctor, doctor, bring me the news of all those goddamned *s*'s.

19

In a conversation about her leg Mom says the doctor says Nonno's kidneys seem
    to be giving out.
Ninety-two next week.
Cars falling harsher down and uphill than the phone ringing.
Do wop de bop.
Like a little prayer no end and no beginning.
Doctor thinks they will check again in three months.
Mom says Nonno says nothing of a pain or going to the toilet.
L'uccello del cielo (four to seven high thin notes) doesn't sow and doesn't reap.
Likewise the book of life.
A common resident west of the Sierras.
Be bop de beep.

20

All is changed, changed utterly.
Torso rotated in stone, wolves frozen in a snarl at a hand once made them
    wolves again.
We concede the fourth and fifth argument.
And whether it is a terrible beauty or a question of no more heart up the sleeve.
And whether those born without any ever find anything proximate besides.
The book is knowledge of a life.
Or some conjugation of Satanic teachings with an emphasis on mutilation with
    steel objects.
Consequently, our conclusion is the same as before.
All those *s*'s the heart dragged in.

21

Jay sends pine needles off the roof past the window looking for something
    belongs to him.
At 9:57 a quake, followed by a strong aftershock at 10:23.
To *blank* where the *blank* never did.
In between a hummer came to hang near my face until another dove at him
    from above.
This is clear from what has been said previously.
On the phone during the second jolt with an Italian translator in New York had
    to say, Excuse me, there is an earthquake.
Busy morning, even in Italian.
She talking of the shock of Adriano's death followed by Antonio's when the
    quake struck.

22

There lay a multitude of impotent folk waiting for the troubling of the water.
De beep de bop.
Arrival and departure should be understood not according to place but according
    to the angels' *turning* to one another.
Phone rings.
Young birds resemble females, some difficult to identify.
A woman named Zebra Brown wants to know if any unemployed persons in my
    household.
Afternoon breeze is up and dry again.
I say No, there is nobody here.
Migrate by day, flying low.
Eggs, 2, are small, white.
When the heart wants in.

23

In the Seventh Article We Ask:
Can We Speak of a Book of Death as We Speak of the Book of Life?
Helmut who spoke much of angels lost his heart June 14 after dinner.
He had had it for 75 years.
Four to seven high thin notes the heat wants in.
His only time in Los Angeles Helmut spoke of those he saw on roller skates
    serving cars at a drive-in on La Brea.
Tanya says a letter came from Helmut the day after he died citing Cavafy:
"Even this first step is a long way . . . "
Hence no comparison can be made.

24

Abraham hath not known us.
To which Augustine adds, 'The dead, even the saints, do not know what the living
    are doing.'
Do wop de bop.
In the wild wild west.
Males have a pendulum courting flight, with distinctive patterns for some species.
Give him to the road, give him the pain makes his life ring again.
Argentine poet who was blind, I think, or dead or committed suicide wrote some
    thing like that.
This Gregory states explicitly when commenting on the verse in Job:
'Whether his children come to honor or dishonor, he shall not understand.'

25

Work is the answer, wrote Baudelaire.
After I dreamed of kissing Becky only to learn *work* is Jamaican for weed as in
    doing any good work lately?
Where is the pure night, wrote Borges, which unlettered day allows?
Consequently, there's no need to posit a medium to carry from one angel to
    another.
I didn't know what time it was.
That's a question, depending on how long you have been watching mockingbirds
    dive at a big yellow dog.
Do wop de bop.
La pura noche.
Who after all needs heart when you have as much work as this?

26

Sailors are skeptical by nature.
There's no question of that soft expanse flagrant to the eye.
Western wind when wilt thou blow.
That's not a question either.
In the wild wild west.
Or in the sense in which we say angels are in place.
Do wop de bop.
Over 2,000 arrests last year in Los Angeles for sex in a moving vehicle.
Mama, ce l'ho lungo.
What Dante might have sung had he not survived.
Along the Harbor Freeway Aphrodite Anasthesia spilled Sprite on a sheaf of
    poems.
That's a question dividing my glance from time to time.
Be bop de beep.
Patterns pretty soon change people and the engines of their writing.

27

Years ago Helmut read on a train above the heating knob *arm und alt*, poor and old, the *w* and the *k* clearly scratched out.
The man up the street people are visiting with briefcases came out twice this morning to spill a pail of gray water down the gutter.
Isn't that strange, wrote Helmut to Tanya in a letter she got the day after he died.
What is more gentle than a wind in summer?
What is more soothing than a pretty hummer?
That's a question, only if love spilled backwards.
The city is empty, empty, empty, Helmut also wrote in that last letter.

28

A woodpecker up the hill for the first time in over a year.
That's not a question.
In angelic speech the *reference* or *turn* required is not one that's known but one that makes known.
Followed minutes later by someone on a piano picking out the chorus to Beethoven's Ninth.
Find is not in my thesaurus though *angel* certainly is.
Tochter aus Elysium.
A mouth anyway around which the world.
n. 1. Spirit, cherub, seraph, principality, virtue.
Or vice versa.
2. *See* MINISTER, DEMON, GENIUS.
De beep de bop.
Or vice versa.

29

God parked his car so that my garbage wouldn't be picked up.
In the Seventh Article We Ask: Can One Angel Speak to Another in Such a Way That Others Will Not Know What She Is Saying?
Or what I thought I heard one of M's friends, a literary theorist, complain to her.
Or vice versa.
Paradox is the devil's workshop.
It is not so much growing old, wrote Helmut, but.
Or vice versa.
In the wild wild west.
Where we keep on moving until beauty is going to find us.
America is a terrible lie, Helmut also said after he died.

30

O Freunde, nicht disse Tone!
When Uncle B was a child he pissed down the furnace grate to vent his rage.
Or vice versa.
Let us sing more cheerful songs, more full of joy!
Or vice versa.
Little B didn't stop, even after they fitted him with glasses.
Time waits. Bud Powell. New York, 1952.
Only to find it rhymes with sorrow.
Tomorrow I read a fortune which says, "Le purgatoire n'est pas artificiel when a yen is just Japanese money."
The same holds true for the seventh difficulty.
Here everything depends on the will of the angel speaking.
Or vice versa.

31

Gardeners with their loud blowers everywhere this morning.
Freude schonner Gotterfunken.
For angelic speech all that is required is a nod or turning to one another.
Fog and breeze and a brief flock of crows with the traffic down and up.
Hummers drain more than a feeder a week now especially.
Street cleaning machine too wheezing down and up the drives and circles.
It's Tuesday, almost 9, the breeze calming as cars go faster.
The man up the street has just come out to sit awhile in his truck.
America qua, America là.
As explained previously this does not happen in angelic speech.

32

Love is a collage turned off and on.
Even if it were noon and almost August a morning breeze seems to linger.
A silken purse applauds the sow's ear.
Or vice versa.
Though that was another time, when computers were monstrosities costing the
    earth, and their circuits you imagined channeled an angel's blood.
Or vice versa.
While there is little heart and only a mouth around which or when who's pulled
    inside out like a silver lining.
The same holds for the difficulty of all those *s*'s.

33

The Book is a mouth around which.
Or vice versa.
I knew I couldn't write of the cat I ran over yesterday wriggling back and front like a worm in my rearview mirror.
Consequently there is no need to posit a medium to carry from one angel to another.
Or vice versa.
Even the Worm can share contentment
And the Cherub stand before God.
Pinched just about in-half with my left rear tire.
Or vice versa.
Answer me who burn with thirst and liquid fire.
Not heard the woodpecker or Beethoven since then.
Do wop de dop.
I seem to see those eyes already.

34

Difference between cats and you on the asphalt is all that paper to fill out.
Be bop de beep.
Or vice versa.
Then into the fire put yourself ahead of me.
That's not a question especially since modernism is dead and the cat scooped up along with all those *s*'s.
Answer me.
An angel is where she operates.
De bop de beep.
When the heart wanted in before any dreams.
Pasiphae enters the cow pure and ready to be mounted to the stars.
We concede the fourth, fifth and sixth arguments and the seven virgins in a little while.
Already I seem to see her eyes.

Book III

Paradise is desolate at the moment; a 'serene and rapturous emptiness,' Yeats called it. In paradise our reporter interviews 21 divorced women and sometimes has dinner with his daughter, S, Uncle B or P. Except for notes and xeroxes from J and letter from Uncle Z, everything else is on the phone.

The sea and sky and you and I.

Sipping his soup he wondered, Who are these fashionable men and women, are they all in search of divorce? And if they are, divorce must be a blessing far greater than wealth for all in this glittering room seem wealthy.

O fair Apollo, want and
bitterness kindle my song.
O swift Python, pollo of circumstance, glide into my breast and seethe there as you did when you sucked me from the skin in which my hymns were sleeved. O rare Apollo, spindle my heart.

"I know men like books," she said, rising, "and you seem a man of your word." (If one were body— and here it's hard to predict how one bulk admits another, which must be if body coins body.)

"Wait, I will prepare your credentials," she added, sweeping out of the room.

Only minutes passed after she had gone, women's laughter reached his ears and he began to feel uneasy again, as just then the maid entered and asked him to follow.

O me in this little boat that
singing makes its way, an
inborn and ready thirst takes him fleet, almost, as a glance to heaven.

He was quiet but desire was on his face and with it the question, hotter than in plain words. All the beautiful women from the restaurant the night before rose to receive him.

Even in his brief stay his mind fastened upon the beauty who spends a million a year in dresses, and gives one to wonder whether the true motion of the clouds may be known by the motion of their shadows.

"May I honor your book with mine?" she asked blushing.

"Certainly," he said, overcome and almost lost.

O Time! Consumer of all things, to say there is no water on the moon.

"I remained cool towards my suitors," she smiled, "for I loved beauty most and knew some of it would be sacrificed to become a wife. Then one day I learned from my mother our fortune was just about gone and I must marry to keep my position.

"And so I chose an old millionaire whose passionate years, I thought, had flown and would spend very little time in my company. But I was mistaken."

Here he saw the Lady so easy passing into celestial light the curtains grew brighter and he was silent.

5

"Realizing he might only enjoy my beauty in the few hours before I retired, while putting on my cream poultices, chin bandages and silk mask, he began to ridicule me, night after night." Poising a finger on the handle of the teacup, she smiled again. "Soon as I gathered sufficient grounds I came to Reno and sued for alimony and divorce. Tonight I'm off to gay Paris."

If a star changes and smiles, what does one become who by nature is subject to every kind of change? As she sipped tea and glanced at her watch, he whispered, "Tell her, tell her!" to himself.

Men and words are ready
made, dear reader, for Truth was the only daughter of Time.

Of the horse or the bird of comedy he will say nothing because he knows the times. Tears fall from the heart and not the brain.

The earlier books found her wings and feet, meaning something else. So one does one's best to bill the humble heart for misunderstood and rejected merchandise, the refuse of so many buyers.

He read she was staying with friends at a cozy flat in the suburbs. When he told her point blank the nature of his visit, she clapped her hands and laughed. "My confession has to begin," she said, "when I left college."

"The little love I had was almost cool, and in six months my mind was made up to leave. To make our parting easy, I began spending money like water until he complained that a wife was a very expensive luxury indeed and gave broad hints he'd had enough. At the end of ten months we parted good friends, never to meet again."

It happens, he thought, when the world comes in upon you it whirls in at the eyes.

"I was free to go without any reason and with alimony of $5,000 a month the rest of my life."

"How to obtain all those nice things," she said, "and remain respectable." (Why did a voice upend his desire?)

"To make a long unpleasant story short, we were married exactly two weeks later and in a year I made life so miserable he was only too glad to be rid of me and all the alimony I asked."

The fire offended. Flies on the eyes at noon.

Tuesday   Wednesday
Thursday Friday Saturday
and Sunday dinner with
Uncle B. Monday Tuesday
Wednesday the head on
top of which the figure
places a hand. A man
when he lies down is a
ninth of his height. Flies
on the eyes at noon. A felled tree which is shooting again. Wednesday Thursday
Friday pick up S after school and dinner. Saturday where the shadow's on her
face still hopeful the earth is a star.

She murmured caressing the roses and lifting her violet eyes, "From that moment, my husband's face became unbearable."

Sunday Monday Tuesday
started the third part,
rosemary bread and tomato salad for supper, Wednesday as far as the leg. Thursday did her leg and at night a pair of broiled pigeons with P. Friday finished the angels in procession with three cracked tin hearts and dinner with S.

11

So he saw the glorious wheel move and render voice to voice with harmony and sweetness that cannot be known but here.

"The rest was easy. When I sued for divorce and alimony, with tears in his eyes the old rancher told all the pranks I played on him to which the judge only laughed as too ridiculous of excuses for mistreating a good wife."

Tuesday night kind of weak and ate some rosemary bread and an omelet and salad. Wednesday fasted. Where the shadows should be on the face. From the chin to the roots of the hair is a tenth of the whole figure. April 1 a Sunday, lunch with Uncle B and at night didn't eat.

Soon as the blessed flame took up the last word he allowed his gaze to wander into the office where the young hotel owner was sitting. Her calm, stern look was fixed on the door through which the newlyweds had disappeared.

She shook her head and with a slight shrug turned to the menu she was preparing. "Poor fools," he hears her murmur.

On the 18th, the night of
St. Luke's, started using
my new blanket. Tuesday
the head of the bending angel and had tomatoes and rosemary bread and B gave me a sonnet. Flies on the eyes at noon. Where a shadow should be on her face.

Imagine, who would understand what he saw now, hold the image, as he spoke, hard as a rock.

From this his eyes recovered to be raised again, and he saw himself translated to a higher dispensation where ornamental rivers flow underground.

Friday started an hour before dawn on the angels' backs. Bread salad for supper with S and Uncle B, asparagus and boiled eggs and it was a beautiful day. Saturday Sunday which was Palm Sunday had good fried pasta at Uncle B's. No tambourines in the garden, says B, no scenes, please, to spoil the makeup.

Here memory pilfers tact and the only two melodies we catch directly: persistence and averages.

"Yes," she nodded, slightly blushing, "there's nothing I'm ashamed of nor wish to hide for it's all a work of faith. Step in, please, and make yourself at home."

He followed into the neatly furnished parlor and took out his notebook. "Don't ask whether I've learned to love another since."

On the 24th at night veal
kidney and asparagus with
P and finished her one leg.
Sunday night two eggs. Monday wrote letters. Spend, O gentle heart, your perfect reader.

Words may seem too stubborn making less of the delight in those eyes where desire found rest.

"Every night, as he put his old spidery arms around my waist, I repented not sticking to my typewriter. I saw very little of his money and was nothing more or less than a bird in a gilded cage."

Thursday a wing. Friday the other wing. Saturday the thigh of the tall smiling one. Sunday dinner with S and Uncle B and in the morning planted two more trees. Thursday the rest of the leg, a spinach omelette and fell asleep on the couch. In kneeling a man loses a fourth of his height.

Glancing over that morning's paper an item on page 16 caught his eye: Prominent Men Fight Over Divorced Woman.

Ivy is a type of longevity, writes Leonardo, and a falcon, time. Friday, the backs. Saturday the big angel and had supper with S and Uncle B. O gentle reader, do not blame me if a point isn't part of a line.
Monday   Tuesday
Wednesday did the hearts in the angels' hands, spinach soup and vodka and woke up at 3 a.m. on the couch. For a book of boats driven against rivers and shadows that were to be her face.

He found the cozy flat. (So, as the Lady warned, put on the flame of your offended fire, practice selling your thirst.) At the door the French maid told him her mistress was out but a twenty in her apron said she would look again.

"It begins when I left Vassar and came back here, waiting in my father's house for what chance may bring in the shape of a husband to pay my bills and hire good servants."

Friday supper with S.
Saturday Sunday Monday
fried beans and spinach, rosemary bread and a bottle of rosé. Tuesday Wednesday night drink with Uncle B.

Silent he followed into a lavish room where the heiress sat by a piano fingering some sheet music. With a nod of her fine head she motioned to a chair.

"I must ask how much you know."

"What I read in the paper," he said. "You married a star about a year ago and recently divorced."

Monday the 4th of July began an angel with legs like this and a letter to T. Tuesday a thigh and the diarrhea's better. Friday night supper with S and P and the diarrhea about over and with it the little pains. Saturday and Sunday had supper and drinks with Uncle B.

19

"After the stroll a dinner followed, and all the time I was breathing heaven on earth. I began to wonder whether he was human or the spirit of some gallant cavalier come back to play with my love's hungry soul."

Already the blessed mirror rejoiced in her words and he was tasting his, tempering the bitter with the sweet.

"The sway of perfection," she smiled and turned her head, "is a series of disgusts."

O gentle reader, you time-
ly dodge, consumer of all
things, Helen now looks at
her great glass and weeps and wonders why she had been twice carried away.

Turn and listen, she told him softly, paradise isn't just in my eyes. Were I now to smile you would be turned like Semele to ashes.

Smiles of women and the motion of great waters. No flies on the eyes at noon. Even if kneeling a loses the fourth part of his height. Wednesday the arm. Thursday. Friday the body and wings. Saturday the thighs. Sunday. A calm stone against which a wave of serpents breaks. Monday Tuesday started her lower back. Wednesday small rain at daybreak. Thursday Friday Saturday. Sunday early dinner with S and Uncle B and didn't go to Mass.

"He was a salesman who came here to dry out and being a clever talker he got my attention." The Lady, with only a lift of her long neck, impelled him up the stairway.

"I rushed straight home from the bank, almost blind with tears and rage, and ordered him out of my hotel. I sued for divorce the very next day."

Friday supper with S and Uncle B and the weather started to clear. Sunday S and I went for a hike and ate fresh bread. Monday up an hour before dawn and did the torso of the child who holds the heart and at night a good birria off a truck for supper.

"I suppose you don't want my real name nor where I was born or educated but, I may as well say, I'm a Vassar graduate ready to meet the world face to face and fight life's battles to win, given half a chance."

And the happy spirits flamed in circles as she spoke, "If it weren't for father's check every month, maybe I'd be home right now, married to our neighbor's son and raising a family."

Monday as far as the hips
and at night it started to
rain. Thursday the thigh and legs. Friday the wing. Saturday the heart next to hers. Sunday up early and did the torso underneath. Monday the shin of her big thigh. Tuesday more rain.

Of places far withdrawn and hours selected from a thousand. Still the blessed fire reft the words as he told them.

And she: "The very next night we dined at Rector's. I set my trap at once with plenty of encouragement but he was bashful. So I made him drink more than was good for him and by 2 a.m. I knew as much of his family as the poor thing did himself. By 3 he had proposed and we were married at 10:30 that morning.

At 11 we telegraphed his father the good news and settled in a hotel, he to sleep off his drunk and I to wait for the storm to break."

Sunday early supper with S and P and a tooth hurt.

Just as the bachelor arms himself and doesn't speak until the master submits the question, he armed himself with every reason as she continued: "Entering the room I found my father-in-law calmly chewing the end of his black cigar. 'Look here, kid,' he smiled, 'you got one over on me this time. You married his money but don't think you're too smart because he has none of it yet. Suppose you tell the young fool the truth, how much is it worth?'

'Two million,' I answered without a blush.

'Done,' his father said, and took me right away to his lawyers where he paid the two million and the expense to have the marriage annulled."

25

At these words the flaming circle fell quiet. He had hardly settled in the chair when a sliding door glided open to reveal an extravagant purple room where on a Turkish divan reclined the most beautiful woman he had ever seen.

Monday argued on the phone with M and N and stayed home all day to draw. Tuesday tried the figure under the wing.
Wednesday the body below the breasts. Thursday her whole leg. Friday it rained, supper with S. Saturday Mom's two gallons of olive oil arrived. Sunday supper at Casita with Uncle B and got drunk.

26

    And he thought, May healing come soon or late, as it will, into these eyes she enters with the fire for which I always burn.
    The light for whom he had spoken circled him three times, he so pleased her with his words.

Monday mutton, salad,
grapes and a pound of
rosemary bread and the head under the big wing. Tuesday Wednesday Thursday Friday dinner and a movie with S. Saturday K stopped by to see how my garden translates a Polish proverb about Time softening the Dick. Or maybe vice versa.

She smiled and lit a cigarette.

"But, madam," he said, "I'm looking to publish confessions not secrets to be guarded as such."

She shrugged her luxurious round shoulders: "The few secrets I have are not like that. They weigh upon me and sooner or later must be shared."

She puffed her fragrant cigarette and began.

Sunday vermicelli for dinner at Uncle B's. Monday the helmet. Tuesday her head like this. Wednesday the torso and at night ate a sandwich. Thursday the wing and an omelette for supper. Friday her body and rabbit with S and P. Saturday her arm and where it rests.

From the last time he had looked up, he saw the whole arc stretch from one end, beyond Catalina, back to that far shore where Europa made herself a sweet burden.

"When I had just turned sixteen and made my debut in society, the newspapers announced me as the most beautiful debutante of the season. My heart was besieged by all sorts and I, being young and inexperienced, treated them all with equal contempt.

She paused to light another sweet cigarette.

Sunday supper with Uncle
B and got drunk. Monday Tuesday Wednesday Thursday Friday worked below her figure far as the corner.

The enamored mind that wooed the Lady more than ever burned to bring his eyes to her.

"Too much petting and attention spoiled my senses," she went on, "until the other girls hinted Father was not wealthy as people supposed, that I had beauty but not enough clothes to make it last.

"Weeping bitterly I went to my mother and made her promise all the clothes I needed even if our home should be mortgaged. Which she did."

And the virtue that look indulged drew him from the dazzling nest of Leda and delivered him into the quick sky.

Sunday and Monday cooked an oxtail and stayed home to draw. Tuesday the wind.

"Desperate," she continued, "they and their mothers gave broad hints I had no jewels which a girl in my position must. I was seventeen now and made to consider marriage the salvation for my wounded pride.

"I gave slight encouragement, thinking him very wealthy, though fifty and homelier than the rest. The next morning came a beautiful diamond necklace with a polite note.

"Weeks went by, he visited often with more jewels until one evening in the parlor he took my hand and placing a big steel-blue diamond on my finger whispered softly in my ear."

Wednesday her torso. Thursday the leg. Friday her head and all the hair and supper with S and Uncle B and P.

A circle of light wheeled by so fast, and this encircled by another and that by a third and the third by a fourth, the fourth by a fifth and then the fifth by a sixth.

Beyond wheeled a seventh, spread now so wide Juno's messenger, in all its arc, is too narrow to contain it. And so the eighth and the ninth.

"'Look,' he said to me, 'the only stone like it in the whole world with a thousand lives and colors all for you.'

"Two weeks later we were married and my love for his diamonds kept me with him a year until he sold the stones to avoid bankruptcy. Our bond was now broken and I sued for divorce.

Saturday Sunday and Monday didn't work.

To have read the particles of that seething light bound by love into one volume.

O how slow this old man wanes, said Columbus or was it Theseus in Cairo or cruising Sunset Blvd. Lamenting the slow moon separating him from Hippolyta.

Four nights will quickly dream away the time, said Hippolyta or was it Melville after his first day of meetings in Hollywood.

Multitudes of blind men, said Melville or was it Columbus, worst city in the world for them.

Monday an omelette and a salad and a certain modesty of speech, half in love, as the odds have it, with easeful death.

Where a single moment, he thought, was more oblivion than thirty centuries since the enterprise made Neptune stare up at Nemo's shadow.
Stop, she whispered, before you make a school out of love.
To those bright eyes he turned his eyes again.

Neighbor up the street
looking better even if a lit-
tle pale in shorts trimming his roses. How do you hold the heart still? says Uncle B. There's gravity for you, says Uncle Z.

Gold Mountain
[1996 - 1997]

Pearl Morton had taken over the upper floors of the Murietta Building some time after Department One of the Superior Court gave up its dignified quarters to move into the red sandstone courthouse which opened in August of 1891. Miss Morton moved in from Marchessault Street, on the Plaza, and so transformed her new establishment that, with its lush dancehall, it became a favorite attraction of male tourists as well as patrons.

A familiar sight to the inhabitants of the courthouse world was that of Miss Morton and a group of her girls carrying tilted parasols and parading through the streets of the area in an open carriage. Sometimes she would vary the procedure and, wearing a gaudy ostrich-plume hat, would herself drive a team of horses, harnessed tandem. Behind her in the cab sat a man blowing a trumpet. Again, she was sometimes accompanied by a white bulldog. All these sights are recalled by still-living ex-judges, ex-lawyers, ex-officials, and ex-businessmen, Angelenos of distinction and of excellent memory.

W.W. Robinson, *Tarnished Angels*, 1961

Is this lot better than box feet?
You are very loud and heavy
Americans and smell like iron
and wear red faces and much hair.
You talk everytime of what you do
even when little wind at sunset
cooling the brick and iron sun
keep moving like yellow dog
tied to post tired of barking
at other dog passing by.
You talk out of big faces
call me pretty woman
and all the money you must make.
You drink so loud enough to sleep
and call me more names with red faces
with crying faces in the dark.
When you sleep I get up to look
in big boots to see money
you promise and never there.
Once big nose dark face man wake up
and my little feet go quick
into his long boots. I say
see my little box feet in you
see me walk like you on Gold Mountain.

"Why all way here to sell it to these english these noisy potato face ask youself, say Caterina Teresa, why not sail other way back to the city you father, to sea where we live more gentle they say than the Gulf everyday more warm and gentle than cold Pacifico; make youself something, Caterina Teresa, don't sit like other girl all Sunday and sing the sad until the customer come, move youself make a picture of you sparkle of sea like other blue sparkle on the ring of you father's big hand; don't sit around funny with other girl drinking Winslow, talking about all fine frock, stop dreaming of him with tall quiet nose; he is gone, Caterina Teresa, gone and safe from the face who come after him at night and call themself police; and he say you have get up and leave this town of dirty angel, and so many thing have happen before men and women like you and him can live together happy; enough, Caterina Teresa, save what you have, stop with the syrup, do what you say at least for him and his and you inside."

June 1, 1897

Dear Henry,
    I just want you to be certain that you know how much you have meant to me! You have been <u>so much</u> of a friend, words cannot say.
    I will never forget how that night I was fretting so you told me to head right home and put my son on his stomach, remember?
    Anyway I will miss you with all of my heart and I really do love your caring about the children and myself for all of these years.
    Please let us not loose touch. I will try to get a letter to you, maybe courtesy of one of our mutual friends, once I have settled in Georgia.

    Love,

    Marge

"	Night ain't nothing to understand, it's Monday, Tuesday, Wednesday, Thursday. Women of the night they say talking to the ladies in church or writing in that paper not fit for a girl even to wipe her ass. Never been the night that's hard but Monday noon or Wednesday at four in dead of summer when you don't want eat or drink or lay around and it's too awful hot and dusty to even think of taking a walk. What with everybody staring if you is walking alone and too damn ignorant to see you want walking like any other body passing the day a little by yourself. Night be when all them's inside except for ones with money or a rich ugly wife, say they got business and they come in after stuffing and drinking themselves redfaced. And then on Sundays take the wives to the ugly little churches all starched and shaved and some nasty righteous little piece who's been poking it in his sow since the sun's come up, all for the greater glory of Jesus' almighty, gets up on the pulpit and starts in on rampant vice and godlessness and how to purify our fair community of sporting houses and the wicked wicked brazen painted women. And he all redface too like the rest doing the weekly duty on the wife and remembering what it was like coming down here. So, Jake Rappett, if this be the news from Lena, Queen of the sporting houses you want, I don't rightly know, though I think it surely worth the case of what you been paying me. All I got to say is that women of the night's a joke on somebody right now.	"

Sunday Midnight

Which half did I get, my daddy's beautiful lying ass or momma's brains? Sure, it's a dumb question that's why I'm only asking myself it here. I mean about my mama and daddy wherever he is probably dead or back up in San Francisco, and she worse than dead back home in the Quarter. I don't blame what they done, making me like this ain't their fault exactly. You know, *like this* being what them bastards up on the hill want to call us, when what they saying is not *like them* raunchy asses dressed up Sundays to hide the cheating and stealing. Who's going to spend her life like Marge blaming her daddy being like he was, no better or worse than God made him, blaming her piss poor luck on him being a coward and nasty and all and her mama not standing up for the girls. So it get her and her kid back home for six months, a year and after that? Most have no place to go back to, so what's a body to blame after all? Ain't blaming anything in this life, least of all what you've got to do. Anyway, few things can help the way they is here and now. Drink all the wine and stuff you can but sooner than later you got to just up and stop or play your hand all the way out once you decide.

                      Me,
                         Pearl

Box feet too smelly in the heat.
Always not enough water to wash
always too many customer to meet
and smile and say how are you
always too much wine to drink
and spill on the floor and say O
very sorry do you like more.
It is too much dust and hot
to have so little water
too many good customer
spend money like syrup on spoon
promise to see me in afternoon
and leave bitter wine. O
he bad customer Madame say
of man in the street with scar
under big Mexican hat O
he tough customer Madame say
of sailor with funny moustache
and tight pants. So many customer
I think so many houses and
saloon make as many emperor
as bottle of bitter wine.
I think I am not emperor
I am tired and maybe go north
and look for two young sister
on Gold Mountain where they are
many more Chinese even if
they not so good customer.

September 17, 1896

Dear Kati,
    Because we are inside a system so thoroughly corrupted, how I wish I could do something good, so as to prove to you that I would like to be less ungrateful for how kind you have been to me.
    Even if most systems carry the signs of oppression, I reproach myself for my cowardice, I ought instead to have defended my books and papers, even if it meant fighting with those police. Others in my place would have used a revolver, and certainly if as a philosopher and a man one would have killed some ruffians like that, one would have been acquitted. I should have done better so, and as it is I have been cowardly and drunk.
    Notwithstanding our treatment as outcasts and the social pressures of even such a crude frontier society as this, I am always filled with remorse, terribly so, when I think of my work as being so little in harmony with what I should have liked to do. I hope that in the long run this will

make me do better things.

So I am writing for your support and your most generous understanding, as you, more than anyone else, must realize the difficulties of my current situation in this pueblo. After all, isn't it just like that everywhere? Business not too good, resources exhausted, people discouraged and as you said, not content to remain spectators, and becoming nuisances from being out of work— if anybody can still make a joke or work fast, down they come all over him.

I believe to succeed out here in the West, in the universe of big ideas, you must have a temperament different from mine that is becoming sick of the *boredom* of civilization. I have so many plans that I hardly dare to undertake them alone. Though I wish it was not so, I am extremely sensitive to what is said of what I do, as to the impression I make personally. If I meet with distrust and suspicion, if I stand alone, I feel a certain void that cripples my initiative.

We should help each other. Two persons must believe in each other, and feel that it *can* be done and *must* be done, in that way they are enormously strong. They must keep up each other's courage.

So, yours in the glorious contradictions and fugitive passions of life, I remain,

Vincent

September 17, 1896

Dear Margie,

I believe I have never suspected you, nor do I now, of having had financial motives, more than is honest and just. You went as far as is reasonable, other people exaggerated. But for the rest, you understand that I do not hold any delusions about love, and what we have talked of and lived on the road remains between us. Since then, things have happened that should not have taken place. I respect in you a sense of duty— I have never suspected, shall never suspect you of anything mean.

Of myself I know this one thing, that is of the greatest importance not to deviate from our duty, and that we should not compromise with duty. Duty is absolute. The consequences? We are not responsible for them, but for the choice of *doing* or *not doing* our duty, we are responsible.

And my own future is a cup that may not pass away from me except that I drink it. Goodbye, good luck on your own difficult journey. You will understand that I trust in the future with serenity, and without one line in my face revealing the struggle in the deepest depth...

Your,
Vincent

October 10, 1896

Dear Kati,

I have made it as far as Monterrey without too many problems. I hope the good weather and luck keep up and I will be able to find my way soon to that city and the important things that must await me.

Sometimes I cannot believe that I am only thirty-five years old, I feel so much older. I feel older *only* when I think that most people who know me consider me a failure, and how it really might be so, if some things do not change for the better. And when I think *it might be so*, I feel it so vividly that it quite depresses me and makes me as downhearted as if it was really so. In a calmer and more normal mood I am sometimes glad that thirty years have passed, and not without teaching me something for the future, and I feel strength and energy for the next thirty-five years, if I should live that long.

You will understand, however, that I must avoid everything that will tempt me to hesitate, and so I must close this here, in flight,

Your,
Vincent

May 15, 1897

Dear Mama,
      Just writing a few lines to let you know things are about set out here with me and little Vincent. I know that maybe I have not told you so but we will be happy to be paying you and Papa a visit and we are real grateful for the invitation and especially for Papa's deciding he wants to see us both.
      I think that for a family to keep together they have to be able to look at the future and remember who is helping who. The past can just weigh a body down and keep you from going out and doing what you need in this world. I come to learn that especially out here, as I have tried very hard to get myself established and make a life for myself and now little Vincent and Vincent too. I mean Vincent's got a life and a good job of his own and is trying to set up his business in San Francisco so he

won't have to travel so much and find little Vincent and me a nice solid home.

So my little trip to visit you all couldn't have come at a better time, what with making ready for the move up North and me about to finish things off here in L.A. and leave this part of my life behind. Again, I am grateful for the invitation, since I know things sometimes are not so easy for you. I am very glad to hear too that Papa is feeling much better and is not fretting so much about our bad luck and his spells and that he is finally ready and willing to see his beautiful little grandson. I am sure you will both be loving him as dearly as I do.

I have to stop now. I have so much shopping and packing to do still for our trip, what with the long train ride and the Georgia summer and all the little surprises we have in store for you and Papa. Guests can't come visiting emptyhanded after all. We are healthy and happy and looking forward to seeing you all soon.

Love,

Marge

All flowers in garden
Lena laugh and cursing
Marge feed baby Pearl drunk
Caterina say big speeches
with dancing hair and neck.
All flowers I listen to
open hands and face
just before soft wind
come like tear down river
with dark let flower talk
some flower sing of other river
where little girl walking
long ago. All my flower
like I secret in box
where many soft color wait
for me to open and look
pale as moon over head
when I dream of all those face
red moon face over me
talk of money talk of wife
talk of what make in life
I close my eye. Courage
Caterina say to me
as I think of my box
and the many color petal
inside like a book with page
I see on other day
in other light like leaf
with life hang in place of wind
at window. Courage
Caterina say about
many color many way
we leave dust and dry wind
and redface customer
and Mrs. Allen Sunday
and take way back to other
happy river that wind like silk
around hip of Gold Mountain.

" Girl all they do is wait for letter, wait for somebody anybody like in jail to write them. Me I never wait. Me Kati as he call me, need no hopes need no wine and medicine. Kati he call me, his faraway one. The time when he write me through Suarez who have to read all part over before he read it back to me in some kind of english. I keep that letter. I try to learn the words make them talk in his kind of language even if I got trouble reading and writing anykind. And now I want to show him, when we together with ours big olive skin boy with beautiful black eyes like the nights we make love, when we faraway where he and mine come from, next to gentle sparkle of sea, dark blue make me remember. No more this piss Pacifico and stink of river they call Los Angeles of Porciuncula. No more worry about who live on what side of river, who halfbreed wholebreed nobreed, if ours inside me— his and mine-- moving right now Sunday night under full redface Angeles moon is some americano. He our, he mine and belong everywhere I be and was and have been, everywhere he come and go now and tomorrow and the day afer that, all places my father and mother was and be. As I look at big pissoff moon like drunk police the night they come after you outside my little window. As I think I dream you tonight and not smèll river. As I talk for me Kati and mine   "

July 5, 1897

Dear Mama,
 I just cannot understand why you write to me and little Vincent the way you do. And he being still an infant, your own flesh and blood, a darling you will love dearly when you have the chance to hold him in your arms.
 Why does it always have to be money and details? Who's done what to who, how much it cost to do this or get there, who's responsible for this part of this and that part of that and how many years it been since all of it happened anyhow? And love, Mama, doesn't it count for something in your books? You know what I learned in this entertainment business, Mama, even in my younger days when I was a little wild and lacked concentration, is that you got to have imagination, see how things are going to be, not what they was or should have been. You got to think big and want big and have luck and love in your life. You can't just sit around

like some kind of bookkeeper and wait for it to happen.

That's the way it is with me and Vincent and little Vincent, on our way to settling down and finding a nice home up North and getting established. I don't see any call for the things you had to say about Vincent or me for that matter or our fine beautiful boy. Besides, if you look at my last letter I nowhere was asking for any kind of charity from you and Papa, especially money I would be about squandering here in Los Angeles like you said I had done with all the rest. Anyhow, once I hear from Vincent and our plans got settled, I thought you and Papa would be wanting to see your little grandson before the big move up North. And surely, there's no way I would be suggesting charity. I was just planning to inquire, once the time was right, about the possibility of a loan from Papa to help with some of the transportation for little Vincent and myself. A loan, mind you, which Vincent will gladly and speedily repay once we are all settled in our home in San Francisco. All just like business, Mama, all on the up and up. If you cannot see the way to understanding that, with your own flesh and blood, I do not rightly know what more there is to say. Except that I remain still as I have been,

Your loving daughter,

Margie

" I must say Mrs. Allen going on like that about our ten little fingers is, pardon my French, a pile of shit. Sitting on her smug ass at the piano, wiggling her fat fingers and talking about how lucky most of us be compared to lots of people and marvelous just to be relaxing here on a Sunday afternoon, dog-tired and hung over, ain't my idea of fun. As I see it, honey— honey's me, after all— it gets to be more and more a matter of biding my time until I can get the hell out of here. Wait a minute. You think when I was saying honey I was talking about you? You and your smoothass voice and long easy fingers? I stopped talking to you when I did what I had to last week, bleeding for you and me and passed out and woke up barely able to walk. Maybe you ought to think about going into business with Mrs. Bessie Allen. Squeezing up there on the piano stool with her, you soft talking speeches at us about our dignity and rights and the new day coming while she playing piano with those fat fingers and collecting our money. Quite a pair you two would make. Anyhow, honey from here on is just for me. Simple old me who's going to beat it on out of here and head north sure as she's talking to nobody but herself. Blah blah blah. Ain't that right, honey? "

Sunday Sunup

Don't know why I leave this except as a word to those who do care enough to be reading it and must be my friends and do rightly understand. Back home where I come from the old mothers tells us that when a man dies he goes west. I ran west when I was not yet a woman and never came to be one thanks to greed and money and wine and drugs and fine christian cheating faces, both men and women I am sad to say. I believe the only way to find the world I thought I was running to years ago is to head even further west where the sun go to sleep like in the old stories. I do that now.

Pearl Wilson

I do no die in this blind river of ghost.
She wait like yellow moon for me in garden.
Hello, how are you, what have you do today.
Talk to me like dry wind, listen me all night
with smell of river saying prayer in dark
dark wall of room with no moon outside
no flower whisper just redface snoring
with boots on. How you been, just fine and me
waiting at window for you river of hair
and dancing neck and me little box feet
in you lap listening to you make speech
listening you hissing lip and rolling tongue
talk all thing you will make away from here.
Hello, how are you bird singing outside
in dry night, how is song not so pretty
because you too want her singing of old song
about moon and sea special tonight with no moon
just dry wind on lip and stink of river
and many trainful of snoring redface
with boots on. Hello, how are you bird
go follow wind and say her little box feet
make speech tonight talk in dark of no moon
in window no head no whisper on you lap.

August 27, 1897

Dear Mama,
    You have no idea what it is like these days to be a woman out here. Nothing is treated so cheap and in my business there is never so much competition as among us women. Men stand everyday leaning in the doorways along Alameda like the Lord Himself fallen out of Heaven. Nobody worries or cries when we take sick and there is nobody to fuss over us and bring us tea or soup but ourselves.
    Of course you are asking yourself why I am writing all this to you, especially after receiving from you hardly the most kind letter in the world. It is just that you and I are very much the same, Mama, not bodies to be staying mad or keep a grudge for very long. And, besides, I am feeling a little lonely in the summer heat and I know it does me good to write to you and get all this off my chest, the same as I am constantly talking to little Vincent like he wasn't an infant and my best little friend

in the whole world.

A woman has got to know what she wants out of life, how she and hers is going to get established in this hard hard world, and not letting nobody use her or take advantage. She has got to know who loves her and does things for her and how family is so important and, like they say, thicker than water. If she makes mistakes when she was young, and God knows there is hardly nobody who has not, some is just luckier than others, she has got to remember to keep doing what she must, not to give up because it will mostly work out and even up in the end. And the babies is why we are here, Mama, and no two ways about it. They are God's greatest reward to us who keep trying hard to take care of our own and not do any harm.

I know I do go on, so I thank you for your patient ear and hope that you and Papa are well, as always,

Your loving daughter,

Margie

" Alone I drink under this tree full of flower, I lift my cup at the big blood moon and say, Caterina Teresa, the moon and you and shadow make three women, drink up, moon is no drinker and the shadow only creep behind you, but with moon as friend and shadow as maid you drink until the morning come and hot sun and you sicker than dog again. The bed like me so empty I waking up as stink from river get bigger with the night wind blow making leaves like noise of gentle sea like smell of waves carry me back to you. Where are the words who fill my heart, where is letter for Suarez to read me to make me fine, to take away sickness every morning as sun come up hard and mean as voice who say you never come back, you dead you runaway to San Francisco, Nevada, New York, Chicago all places I never find you under this tree empty from my bed. I very sorry I complain and say you name and cry a little in the dark, you wild Kati who need always little more courage to feel you smile and you faraway nose on my lip "

" Wish heat be easing off even rain not helping much, turning everything to steam and mud and more bugs than ever. So what you believe, honey, that I got nothing better to do than be writing myself. Don't it beat lots of others who pretend they is actually writing to somebody who's gone disappeared, dead or maybe never gave a shit in the first place. What if I end up talking to you, ain't a damn lot different than Catrina and Marge and they made-up lovers and families and fuck else, and Suzi Boxfeet funny chanting and giggling in that damn language of hers. Not to be mentioning poor righteous Pearl and the kind of thing she ended up writing. I mean I do know Catrina feel deep about her man but he's long gone and ain't coming near if he cares a wit about his neck, no matter how he promise or how sweet them letters or even if she was pregnant with him for almost five month, them whitetrash with masks is still waiting on him and there's no way he's showing his face in this town. Besides he's fucked and got half the girls on the street pregnant with his smoothass ways, you and me and Marge ought to know, so what Catrina be thinking. And speaking of Marge I mean nobody compare with her when it come to letter writing. Her with that prissy schoolmarm voice and uppity manner wanting to read me aloud what she's writing to her mama and papa about herself and all her plans. She saying she going to be visiting back home in Georgia anyday, when her nastyass papa been dead over five years and her mama maybe dead or at least not written in almost half as long. Got to hand it to her, nothing stops her from making it all up right down to some second child she got with Catrina's Vincent, if one brat ain't enough in this life, you know calling him little Vincent and how smart he is like his father and wanting to head to Georgia and meet the whole dead family. So you ease on up a little, honey, and leave the talking to me if you be having so many scruples. Ain't so bad going on like this and a lot cheaper than wine and Winslow and now you be sleeping almost as good. "

Hello Monday afternoon,
why you look at me like that.
So afraid soon she taking
long road to Gold Mountain
morning come I back to sleep.
I take hand in dream
and ask her say some thing.
I miss you much she say
and no one here send to you
with letter so I send little song
and no talk of redface moon
or weather. I sing her three times
and maybe all line seven
so bright make every word ring
like gold rose when knocking come
Doong Doong on door and find me sleep
in river of you hair

" If that's what people be thinking of you, honey, that you don't exactly give a damn, they be pretty much right. Even your mama used to say to watch out for people cause they pulling you down and making life miserable with they goddamn looks and whispers. Except for them that cares and respects, them you do think about. Like that good easy man up north got hisself caught in the bottle and them wild ideas. Or poor Pearl with her big slow eyes how she turn to you and want you to cut the shit and be talking to her straight and nobody else. Was and still is too many stupid mean God-fearing people in the world for the likes of Pearl. Anyway, past is past as they always fond of saying in this dusty stinking town, so how's about getting on with it, honey? Sometimes I think it were a damn lot better to be like Suzy Boxfeet not understanding half of what people be saying to you and grinning and answering O how you do mista boss, and then up you, pig, bowing in her own foreign talk. Like when she's chirping to herself and mumbling looks as if she ain't even here for that matter, just floating over the dust and crap with them little feet barely moving. Well, you know, honey, I ain't one to be chirping and floating. The Santa Ana been blowing almost a week and all them around the pueblo saying it's mighty strange almost in March and now it be giving me an idea. What if tomorrow morning or Wednesday or Thursday I strolls up Alameda with a bag of clothes like on my way to the Chinese and crosses over to the station and gets on a train heading north. Just like that. Desert wind blowing and my skin shining and I just stepping on out. Secret like that almost worth keeping or ain't it, honey? "

March 7, 1898

Dear Henry,

    I just don't know what to say. Your very wonderful and generous offer has taken me completely by surprise. What with having to postpone our little family excursion to Georgia this Spring, it was going to be a disappointing time for me and mine. Now, that is all going to be different.
    There are so very many things going through my head as I sit here with pen in hand, I do not truly know where to start. My heart tells me to say yes and again yes, but my mind, being what it is, cannot find a handle. It is surely not that what you are proposing is at all outlandish or, God help me, in any way improper, it is just, and I want to be honest with you here, a little unexpected. Since I have not seen you in a while, I thought that maybe you were just too busy or been away on some business or in my silly moments believed that you wouldn't be wanting to visit

anymore. Now I know and understand, that it is my stupid little head with nothing better to do than running after its own tail like some puppy dog.

So, my dear Henry, the answer is of course yes from the bottom of my heart. Your terms, I must tell you, are as fine and upstanding as the man you are. So, it is most definitely the right thing to be wanting a simple yes or no from me and leave the rest to talking face to face when you come to town at the end of the month. I am so excited I don't rightly know what to do with myself. I hope these two weeks won't be dragging on like months as I wait for you and your kind smile. And just think, when I was on the train passing through Riverside on my way out, I never imagined the name of that town could end up meaning so much.

I am now heading right over to Temple Street to mail this letter and begin my wait for you, as always,

With warmest love and regards,

Margaret

"Listen now, Caterina Teresa, some saying you have no feeling other you have too much, while you miserable and ache for him waiting in this ugly stupid. And why you wait, say yourself, is just him or is it new life with him and his and yours? And what so new, Caterina Teresa, be no more redface and sloppy drunk and police with fat nasty hand touching and calling pretty woman? And what you want, to be no more like other girl, no more fight, no more cheat, no more Winslow and bad wine and walk down street in evening with little Suzy or Lena and not hear pig call from shadow or upstair window? And how you think it be different anyplace else like San Francisco even if it not so dusty or dry or stupid americano like here that soon you start acting good housewife as Marge or big businesswoman like pig Mrs. Allen. Here everybody all the time going someplace, every week new place they looking for. So what you do, Caterina Teresa, take little Suzy and change houses like Mrs. Morten offer in fancy new on Plaza or run away up north and look for Vincent and Suzy sister and live wild as you want with you little east moon. Maybe better say it fiesta this week and you taking ride over river to watch a little with Suzy and Lena (Lena understand) and make move to Morten and then ask week or two for trip to San Francisco. It feel like time. Little move first, and stop wish and hope and wait for. What you say, Caterina Teresa?"

Book VI

I wait on you in shadow
say here you little east moon
bring me into Morton house
take care of you like maid
wash iron gown fix hair
for all big shot who visit.
I wait tonight in shadow
watch until you done
and hear my word come you
like funny little wind
from way across river
sing of new day old day
when all together and no hurt
no redface gold and smell
no mountain of howdee
big man big woman sir
no chink and dago nigger breed
no allow be together in big house
just you beautiful long neck
and my little word. Please
I in shadow with no stocking
and wait you lift up crystal curtain
and see you pale east moon
come late tonight sing please

April 22, 1898

Dearest Henry,

    Let me say right off that I am sorry about the things I mentioned in my last letter especially involving the wedding. And although what you said in return hurt me some, your anger was justified by my impatience and silliness.
    I did not mean to be ungrateful and do understand a simple ceremony is best and proper for a couple in our situation. Also, it is only right that Riverside ought to be our wedding site since we will be making our life together there. The idea of a ceremony down here in Los Angeles was just a flight of fancy on my part, something I did not think out well enough. It was probably just a case of being my old persnickety and nervous self trying to please too many people and what with the extra wait and all.

You are a good and righteous man, and I know I couldn't be luckier in this life. Everything is packed and I have moved into the hotel as you said, and am now awaiting your go-ahead.

My deepest love and regards,

Margaret

" Ain't worth it, I says to him, you ain't worth it I whispers at his clean shaven uppity smugass lawyer face as I turn and keep heading down Temple. Nerve of him wanting another free Sunday when last time he wouldn't have got nobody off if it weren't for poor Pearl standing up for me in front of that judge. Not seen the bastard in almost six months and he try giving me that goddamn smile and sweeping his hat off. I mean ain't he just like the rest right now, world full of crazy people who don't give a shit about nobody but they mean ass selves. Should have invited him on over tomorrow to do a threesome with me you and Mrs. Allen. Yes sir, fat Sister Allen at the piano and him trying to take her from behind whiles I clap and keep time. Thought of them going at each other be too nasty to bear, and you know we seen all kind. Now hold on a simple minute and just listen to yourself. Time you stop chattering and be taking steps to grab a train anyplace other than here. Nothing here with poor Pearl gone, Catrina off to Morton's fancy house and little Suzy left behind pining away and shuffling around late at night like some damn ghost. I mean you can't even talk to the new girls, they so dumb and high all the time they barely remembers what you say to them from one day to the next. It's the season to be out of here, honey, before summer come on madder than a yellow dog. And stop calling me honey, you ain't sweet to nobody not even you old self. "

Book VII

Yessiree Mistah Crow
you too waiting for moon
last night of redface year.
I walk and leave sign
like this
      o

and that
      ●

who say you little boxfeet
sing river of ghost for you
come back in new monkey year
to whispering of word
save you from blind water.
No sirree not funny
like you Suzy and dry song
scratch scratch at river
tonight for sound of moon
on me like falling hair.
Yessiree Mistah Crow
how you do with dark
better little old song
than time on Gold Mountain.

Recent Poems
[1999 - 2000]

AMAZON

> "He died very peacefully in the middle of writing a sentence."
>
> in memoriam Morris L. West

A big fish even if all is not so well.
Or a great big river brushing the clouds
when not mired in the not so fragrant plain
like angry weather. Or angry weather
which comes from the Latin to bind
or bring together as in a spiritual endeavor
or enterprise rising like a fleet of
gleaming masts o'er the bounding seas.

Somewhere the other night in sleep we might call Winsome, you know, a north and south of town, dusty pickups, goats and chickens and railroad tracks in the south, while the north end on something like a mesa, green on top, but more an upside down pyramid of earth. Sat at a dusty table under a bougainvillea sipping a beer asking the local preacher how many feet to the top and what keeps north Winsome standing straight up like a frozen tornado dotted at the top with lawns and little white houses. Can't remember exactly how it was said, the one word *center* he pronounced made me look up again and marvel and sip more beer.

Curious what comes to mind with water never seen
or a moon chiming not so brightly.
Again, whether you think so or not,
will never gleam with the heat of a secret rose
a petal played with fingers along a scar.
Amazing what it might more easily be called
if it weren't for that plain that weather
those highways connecting up north and south
and just about anywhere flagrant in between.
Dust, envy and great big fish are qualities of age
and aging as gracefulness remains a gift
of little else than wonder or wanting to begin again
to turn one more time, the gleam in someone's eye
the sleep a little more south or sooner than expected.

ORIENT EXPRESS

Let me introduce the Gilberts of winter
insisting after coffee I wouldn't understand
who smile and most politely call for the check
while finishing their little story of sailing up the Nile
after forlorn departures from Vienna and Budapest,
not to mention a chilly Istanbul almost bereft of caviar.
Take the pencil-thin moustache deleted this morning,
fresh gothic brows for the winter afternoons of Cairo,
their accents nearly impossible to place
amid the sheen of purple and crimson velours
these drear nights when talk of Duveen or Tesori
lingers at table like a dormant Havana.
You know it can only mean something
if the vague insults are forgotten by morning
along with the defeated moustache or lace collar,
if the name of the dead boy is identical
to a street down the block from that quaint city hall
where a movie about psychics may be shot next summer.
So now it's just a matter of getting it down quicker
telling the popular from what only seems inspired,
the bang and the burp and the burr under the saddle,
all the little voices left over since childhood
was imprinted in comic strips, in cartoon exile
of sleepy orange orange trees and flat hippopotami,
natives native to baggy pants and losing cigars.
Who are you, you say, to ask whodunit
to question the confidence of the Gilberts
to listen for the anger behind their dexterity
no matter the pleasure or how far they've come.
The Gilberts are always waiting traveling smoking
ordering another cognac champagne martini
a salad nicoise just before dinner
they don't have the least intention of eating.

CHRISTMAS 1999

The answer of course would come out of Nevada.
It didn't begin as a question of good or evil
though something like a demon figured in rumors.
Photos reveal that her rather pretty face was untouched.
Most of the victims, we soon learned, had been young women.
People regard the sheriff as a quiet, nice enough fellow,
more than a little disturbed by events at the monastery.
The odd thing remains the monks' almost stubborn reticence.
As if there's not much to do, nothing really to understand,
just a matter of resolve and letting events take their course.
Most people consider the sheriff right for the job.
Methodical to a fault, he keeps visiting the monastery:
easing out of his car, smiling against the keen winter light
more like a tourist pleased with an unseasonably mild December;
while the abbot squints, looks down, finds a tired smile
anxious, it seems, to get back to the mercy of his library.
All in all, events contradict the fine desert mornings,
some sense of mystery and dread implicit in the question.
Everyone agrees there are no immediate answers.
It's become a problem of character, of waiting and watching,
as if all hint of direction points to its opposite.
Very little information seems readily available.
Procedure follows procedure, comparisons deny comparison,
walls and hoof prints and books should be made to talk.
For now these questions demand a more sustained position,
something besides a famished moon, stars without twinkle
or the late morning glare peeled back for the purest of reasons.

Spring Again

Even with mounting inflationary pressures,
the relentless etiquette and aspirations
alongside almost global indifference,
whether or not capital is lyrically suspect
and might easily take us for a ride.
Oh well, it's time to write of spring,
lithe thighs mispronounced,
something-in-the air rectitude longing for it,
resenting the old news out of Nevada,
Malnevada of lowghost grandfathers
who left it all behind for job and cigar.
O the faces, O the wobbly instinct
the breezy light unfurling
squirming little green, yellow and white flags
strung between the fried chicken place
and lampposts in the parking lot.
Nothing out of place despite our interest
in a snapshot facing downhill
almost at the top of a dead end street
just north enough of Chinatown.
Oh well, late afternoon and this
desire, in a word, suspicious
of every modesty one may sue for
with passing spring again and sincerity.

*

She awoke offended by her pillow
rumpled there in rudeness.
That Beethoven might write a toccata for piano.
Heat in late May, spring already lost
to the tyranny of latitude
hint of ripe buzzing unquiet in the breeze.
A pallid kind of stillness
moisture lingering on the neck
where nobody's seen any ghosts
except lost thoughts and bright ambitions
haunting each glimpse at noon
of something infinitely ruder and more quiet.

O Maia Majesta, mother of dance and wildfire
leave me here the slightest birdsong
and take whatever else you can.

*

A cooler morning and shadows,
what comes and goes who listens,
the smallest wren enlivened
twittering beneath the mocker's rant,
the logic of summer a little abated,
this green still sincerely green,
glistening leaves swaying to butterflies,
quickening branches and nodding boughs
now dance to something not quite here.

*

Sincerity a thought in spring
best left to dreaming,
folded paper towel in the pocket
of a dead man's pant's
now almost two years gone.
And tonight in sleep he stands
behind a row of windows scowling
or maybe just disappointed
moving left to right
one frame to the other following me.
Is it so curious if the dead
like dogs and cats
have nothing to do but us,
our love our terror their only agency?

*

The human animal in June is just a care.
Who signals what or vice versa.
Cocktail sign starts flickering like a candle.
Everybody looking hither and tither.
The night almost warm and satisfying.
Friday has filled all the outside tables.
Few weeks left of spring, the market again rising.
Unemployment, prosperity, all the likely signs.

There isn't even one furious man in the corner
looking out on the street sipping coffee.
Here I wait for you, it seems like years.

*

The comedy of spring is just so
scribbled on a patio over traffic
at the end of a most perfunctory day.
Somebody's father dies at 92 in New Jersey,
who certainly was fine last week,
cooking a roast chicken with carrots,
going to the hospital for nothing
and never coming out.
Is this the way the poem ends?
That comedy remains comedy,
the rest nearly impossible.
If only to wake to anything but mockers.
O chalk-white butterfly O peeping wren
waiting for cat black fur to pass.

PORTFOLIO

Written between 1975 and 1976, this book originally opened with a longer piece of verse and the subtitle "A Novel of Detection". Though later dropped, the subtitle captures the sense of meticulous concentration inherent in the series of the "Events" here, as well as characterizes the longer work in the intervening book such as *Pearl Harbor*, *Tender Continent* and *The Extravagant Room*. It also hints slightly toward the use of collage which again occurs as a form of constraint, forcing attention on new perceptions rather than simply affirming any chance encounter or confusing freedom with the perception that one is free. The question of audience, along with the issue of intellectual property and authenticity, and the concern with the relationship between reader and writer, gradually slips from the foreground in the books that follow *Portfolio*.

ANOTHER YOU

Following *Portfolio*, two books of visual poetry appeared, both written in 1977. These collages were composed primarily of images from magazines and interspersed with newsprint. *Another You* opened with a visual poem made in a similar vein, the image of a flapper presented only by her clothing, jewelry and hat. The face was composed of stock quotes. Another visual work was included, "The End of the Game", although this time the pieces were a collaboration between Italian artist Giulia Niccolai (who contributed idiosyncratic photos of typewriters), the typographically oriented visual poetry of Adriano Spatola and the typed words of Paul Vangelisti. This work had previously been exhibited and performed at the LA Louver Gallery and at UC Berkeley, both in 1978. The poem "Scapes" that opened the book ends curiously in the utterly lost language of Etruscan, a gesture that seems to suggest what can happen when poetry is divorced from immediate context. Similarly, content appears the result of context: a few other pieces in this book were collaged, one entirely from previously written lines original to the poet. The typographical gestures, some of which included striking out lines, added a sense that the previously used language was only growing more tentative, that a search for even wider range of styles was in order.

ABANDONED LATITUDES

This book was another collaboration of sorts. Three Los Angeles poets contributed work that most likely would not have found publication otherwise, much of it organized more or less around geographical themes: John Thomas contributed a piece called "from Patagonia". Robert Crosson whose previous work was already quite geographical contributed a piece called "Wet Check", a work as L.A. based as one can imagine. Vangelisit's contribution include another series of visual pieces called "Reading the Masters" (composed in 1979) as well as two moderately long poems that continued what the novels-of-detection had begun in the way of incomplete fictions. "MVCCLH" (written in 1980-1981) picks up the idiom of Hollywood westerns with appearances by Crazy Horse (who sounds as though he's been reading Henri Bergson), while "Gof in Singapore" (written one year later) takes the West Coast detective fiction style even farther. These two poems are the last and longest of the individual poems to be published in book form until this current volume.

ALPHABETS

The five long poems in this collection were written over two decades, each one organized around the Roman alphabet, an arbitrary but thoroughly entrenched order that allowed the poet to explore personal and ideological concerns concomitantly. The book was arranged in chronological order, beginning with "Los Alephs" (1986), followed by the elegy "Alephs Again" (1988), moving on to alphabetical history "A Life" (1991). The fourth poem "The Simple Life" (1993) is a bestiary that chronicles the lives of friends and literary influences. "Rhum" (1995), the concluding piece, is a double-alphabet and musical sequences of 52 parts in which the poet meditates on number and evil.

BIBLIOGRAPHY

[Poetry]

Alphabets, 1986-1995 (Littoral Books, Los Angeles, 1999)
A Life (collages by Don Suggs, ML & NLF, Milano, 1997, bilingual)
Luci e colori d'Italia (collages William Xerra, Corraini Editore, Mantova, 1996, bilingual)
Nemo (Sun & Moon, Los Angeles, 1995)
The Simple Life (etchings Giuliano Della Casa; Roberto Gatti Editore, Modena, 1992, limited ed.)
Villa (Littoral Books, 1991)
Alephs Again (Red Hill, Los Angeles/San Francisco, ltd.ed., 1990)
Domain: Works-in-Progress (Red Hill, 1986, with G.T. James & photos by Joe Goode)
Rime (drawings Don Suggs, Red Hill, 1984, ltd.ed.)
Abandoned Latitudes: 3 Los Angeles Writers (Red Hill, 1983)
Ora blu (Telai del Bernini, Modena, 1981, ltd.ed., bilingual)
Another You (Red Hill, 1981)
Un grammo d'oro (Cervo Volante, Rome, 1981, bilingual)
Portfolio (Red Hill, 1978)
Remembering the Movies (Red Hill, 1977, collage & text, ltd.ed.)
2 x 2 (Red Hill, 1977, collage & text, ltd.ed.)
La stanza stravagante (Edizioni Geiger, Turin, 1976, bilingual)
The Extravagant Room (Red Hill, 1976)
Pearl Harbor (Isthmus, San Francisco, 1975)
Il tenero continente (Edizioni Geiger, 1975, bilingual)
The Tender Continent (Chatterton's Bookstore, Los Angeles, 1974, ltd.ed.)
Air (Red Hill, 1973)
Communion (intro. George Oppen, Red Hill, 1970)

[Translations]

Amelia Rosselli's *War Variations* (Green Integer, Los Angeles, 2001)
I Novissimi: Poetry for the Sixties (co-ed. & trans., Sun & Moon, 1995)
Adriano Spatola's *Material, Materials, Recovery of* (20 Pages/Sun & Moon, 1993)
Foresta Ultra Naturam: Villa, Niccolai, Caruso (ed. & trans., Red Hill, 1989)
Antonio Porta's *Invasions* (ed. & trans., Red Hill, 1986)
Vittorio Sereni's *Algerian Diary* (Red Hill, 1985)
Corrado Costa's *The Complete Films* (Red Hill, 1983)
Mohammed Dib's *Omneros* (Red Hill, 1978)

Antonio Porta's *As If It Were a Rhythm* (Red Hill, 1978)
Adriano Spatola's *Various Devices* (Red Hill, 1978);
Rocco Scotellaro's *The Sky With Its Mouth Wide Open* (Red Hill, 1976)
Giulia Niccolai's *Substitutions* (Red Hill, 1975)
Corrado Costa's *Our Positions* (Red Hill, 1975)
Adriano Spatola's *Majakovskiiiiiij* (Red Hill, 1975)
Vittorio Sereni's *Sixteen Poems* (Red Hill, 1971)

[Editor]

L.A. Exile: Guide to Los Angeles Writing, 1932-1998 (Marsilio, New York, 1999)

The Promised Land: Italian Poetry, 1975-1995 (Sun & Moon, Los Angeles, 1999, with LuigI Ballerini)

Amiri Baraka's *Funk Lore* (Littoral Books, Los Angeles, 1996)

Transbluesency: Selected Poems of Amiri Baraka/LeRoi Jones, 1961-1995 (Marsilio, 1995)

Italian Poetry, 1960-1980: from the Neo to the Post-Avantgarde (with Adriano Spatola, Red Hill, 1982)

BreathingSpace 79 (cassette anthology of sound poetry, Black Box, Washington, D.C., 1979)

New Polish Poetry (U. of Pittsburgh Press, 1978, w. Milne Holton)

Specimen 73 (catalog of Southern California poetry, Pasadena Museum, 1973)

Anthology of L.A. Poets (Red Hill, 1972, w. Charles Bukowski & Neeli Cherkovski)

Co-editor & founder of literary magazine *Invisible City* (with John McBride, Los Angeles/San Francisco, 1971-1982)

Editor & publisher of *Ribot: the annual publication of the College of Neglected Science* (Los Angeles, 1993-1999)